CHOICE
in
PUBLIC EDUCATION

CHOICE
in
PUBLIC EDUCATION

Timothy W. Young and Evans Clinchy

FOREWORD BY SY FLIEGEL

Teachers College, Columbia University
New York and London

Published by Teachers College Press, 1234 Amsterdam Avenue
New York, New York

Library of Congress Cataloging-in-Publication Data

Young, Timothy Wallace.
    Choice in public education / Timothy W. Young, Evans Clinchy.
        p.   cm.
    Includes bibliographical references and index.
    ISBN 0-8077-3201-X.—ISBN 0-8077-3200-1 (pbk.)
    1. School, Choice of—United States.   2. Public schools—United
States.   I. Clinchy, Evans.   II. Title.
    LB1027.9.Y68   1992
    371'.01—dc20   92-18256

ISBN 0-8077-3201-X
ISBN 0-8077-3200-1 (pbk.)

Printed on acid-free paper
Manufactured in the United States of America

99 98 97 96 95 94 93 92   8 7 6 5 4 3 2 1

To James W. and Sarah A. Daily *for everything*
To Ross, Elayne, Sean, Estelle, Gavin, Vanessa
and
Evans Russell and Sarah Chanil Clinchy
for inspiration and in the hopes of better school days

Contents

Foreword

For those of us who have been involved over the past 20 or so years in attempting to revitalize and, indeed, to re-create the American system of public education, it comes as no surprise that the idea of *public* school choice has emerged as one of the most powerful means of creating that new and vastly improved system of public schooling.

As the authors of this book ably point out, we are—and should always be—talking about insuring that parents have a choice of the *public* school they want for their children, and that our professional staffs, our teachers and principals, have a choice of the kind of schooling they wish to practice.

This does not mean, of course, that our non-public schools should disappear. What the authors of this book, along with many others of us, are arguing is that the same kind of choice that is available to those who can afford it in the private schools should also be available to all parents and students who use the public schools. We should thus be thinking essentially in terms of a strictly *public* voucher system that enables parents to choose the public school they believe will best fit the educational needs, talents, and interests of their children. What we should *not* be doing is diverting any of our grossly limited financial resources from our beleaguered public schools to lend further financial support to those parents who can already afford private schooling.

And speaking of a diversity of different kinds of schooling, if we have learned anything over the past 20 years it is that there is no single kind of schooling that fits the educational needs, talents, and interests of all children and young people. Just as there is a great diversity of needs, talents, and interests in our enormously diverse student population, there must also be a broad diversity of different approaches to schooling in our public schools. There must be a school to fit every student, a system of public education in which no student gets lost and in which every student can succeed.

However, as the authors of this book carefully point out in their review of the research literature and their three case studies, not even educational diversity and public school choice, by themselves, are going to provide that new and better system of public education. In order for diversity and choice to exist in any school system, that school system must be reorganized in such a way that every school has the administrative autonomy to become the kind of school its teachers and parents wish it to become. Teachers, principals, and parents must have the power to design from scratch and operate the unique schools they feel will best serve at least one segment of the student population. They must have the authority to implement their own particular education philosophy, their own curriculum, their own pattern of school organization, and be able as well to select their own staff and control the way the school spends its money.

But even if these three necessities of diversity, choice, and autonomy are present, there is still the overriding concern of making sure that every public school system is first and foremost providing all parents and students with educational equity, that no student is ever discriminated against because of race, ethnic background, gender, or financial need. Diversity, choice, and individual school autonomy must in all cases be limited and controlled to make sure that equal opportunity is provided for every student.

The authors of this book are also careful to point out that the massive changes in our public schools that are brought about by diversity, choice, autonomy, and guaranteed equity are not going to appear full-blown overnight in any school system. The book's case study of Richmond, CA, demonstrates clearly the dangers of inadequate planning, of not giving everyone affected by such changes—parents, teachers, principals, and just plain citizens—a chance to be involved in thinking about and implementing those changes.

Thus the last part of this book is devoted to a detailed description of one tried and successful way in which school districts can go about the step-by-step process of gradually and carefully introducing the combined ideas of diversity, choice, autonomy, and equity.

And finally, the authors take up the ultimate question of how these massive changes must and can become the heart and soul of local, state, and national educational policy, since without their gradual acceptance at all three of these political levels, that new and vastly improved system of public education is not going to be created.

In short, the authors of this book have ably set forth the arguments in favor not only of public school choice but of the three other absolutely necessary components of educational reform—diversity, autonomy, and equity. We can only hope that the message they are sending is heard all across this land.

On a more personal note, I have known Evans Clinchy for many years: He has been an educational visionary who has really changed the lives of children and teachers in a most positive way.

Sy Fliegel

Acknowledgments

We would like to thank the public school teachers and administrators of Lowell, Massachusetts, Montclair, New Jersey, and Richmond, California, whose willingness to share their time and knowledge made this book possible. In Lowell, Lee Ann DeVincenzi, Rosemary LeBlanc, Tom Malone, Jim Neary, Mary Nugent, Beth Scott, and George Tsapatsaris; in Montclair, James Bender, Michael Chiles, David Gidich, Loren James, Joanne Monahan, Jeanne Parker, Frank Rennie, Stephen Rowe, and Tonnes Stave; and in Richmond, Al Acuna, Robert Cone, Doreen Covell, Robert Dycus, Sheila Farley, Bob Heller, Jennifer Jennings, Linda Lister, Don Novak, Deborah Pearce, Pat Rotelli, James Storer, and Susie VanDeVeer.

Other individuals who provided assistance and encouragement include Michael Alves, Frank Brow, Joseph Carey, Roland Charpentier, Elisabeth Allen Cody, Don Davies, Charles Glenn, Owen Heleen, James Hennes, Peggy Hunter, Judy Miller, Joe Nathan, Mary Anne Raywid, Raymond Rose, and Grace Whitaker.

Evans Clinchy would also like to thank his early mentors: the late Theodore Morrison of Harvard University, Carl Lindstrom of the late Hartford, Connecticut *Times*, Cyril G. Sargent of the Harvard Graduate School of Education, Harold B. Gores of Educational Facilities Laboratories, and William H. Orhrenberger, former superintendent of the Boston Public Schools. Tim Young would like to thank the Faculty Research Committee at Central Washington University, which awarded him a research grant.

We also want to thank the New England Center for Equity Assistance and *Phi Delta Kappan* for letting us use previously published material in Chapters 6 and 7 and the Lowell Public Schools for providing the material on the parent information center in Appendix D.

Authors need good editors, and we are no exception. We want to thank Brian Ellerbeck at Teachers College Press for his encouragement, support, and editing skills.

Lastly, we would like to thank our wives, Harriet Drakos Young for her patience and love, and Blythe McVicker Clinchy, without whose love, support, and companionship neither this book nor anything else would have been written.

Introduction

The national debate on school choice has caught the attention and interest of politicians, business leaders, and the public. Policymakers, analysts, and entrepreneurs are flooding the educational marketplace with a multitude of choice proposals that include vouchers and tuition tax credits, magnet and alternative schools, postsecondary and "second chance" options, intradistrict and interdistrictwide plans. Making sense of the debate can be a daunting task for parents and school professionals who may be interested in school choice but are unsure as to which of the various proposals, if any, hold promise for their school, community, or state.

In an attempt to make sense of the debate on school choice, we have written *Choice in Public Education*. As the title indicates, public school choice, rather than nonpublic school choice is the focus of the book. We decided to concentrate on choice in public education for several reasons. First, most of the books written on school choice have focused on choice outside of public education (e.g., Chubb & Moe, 1990; Kearns & Doyle, 1991; Kirkpatrick, 1990; Lieberman, 1989; Rinehart & Lee, 1991). Very few books have dealt in any depth with choice in public education (Nathan, 1989).

Second, much of the debate on school choice has been largely theoretical. We wanted to move from theory to application and contribute a useful book for parents and school professionals who might want to implement choice in their schools, districts, or states. To that end we have reviewed the research on public school choice and identified effective and ineffective options and plans currently in practice around the country.

Third, we chose to concentrate on choice in public education because public schools are where the vast majority of America's children attend and will continue to attend in the future. Although nonpublic schools have a role to play in the education of America's children, that role is and always will be a secondary one. The country's economic, social, and political well-being is dependent upon a healthy and strong public education system.

We have arrived at our interest in public school choice from different directions. One of us has been active in public alternative education for the last 10 years, writing and teaching about individual public schools of choice. The other has spent the past 25 years working in and with urban public school systems around the country, assisting them in the development of magnet schools and "controlled" choice desegregation plans.

The book is organized into seven chapters. Chapter 1 provides an overview of choice in public education, including the arguments for choice, and descriptions of the various choice options and plans. Chapter 2 reviews the research on public school choice and identifies effective choice options and plans currently in practice. Chapters 3, 4, and 5 are case studies of three school districts visited by the authors during the 1989-90 and 1990-91 school years. The three districts (Richmond, California; Lowell, Massachusetts; and Montclair, New Jersey) were chosen for study because all had implemented systemwide choice plans but with varying degrees of success. Chapter 6 details a step-by-step planning process for parents and school professionals interested in implementing systemwide choice in their local school districts. Chapter 7 concludes with a look at the future of choice in public education and a discussion of the larger issue of school improvement and educational reform.

We believe that public schools choice is *the* catalyst for significant and positive educational change. We have written this book to argue for choice in public education and to provide an initial guide for school systems that wish to begin the process of school improvement and educational reform. It is our belief that through the adoption of choice and the structural changes that must accompany it, public education can have a bright and powerful future. We hope this book contributes to that future.

CHAPTER ONE

The Call for Choice

It's time for a second great wave of education reform—not helter-skelter, not here and there, but everywhere—in every state, in every district, for every school and every student in America. These good and tested reform ideas of recent years must become universal—universally understood and applied, and thus universally enjoyed by our children.

Certainly among the most promising of these ideas—perhaps the single most promising of these ideas—is choice. It responds to a simple but quite serious problem. In most places around the country . . . students are arbitrarily assigned by their school systems to a single public school. If that school is a bad one, its students are trapped. Their parents have no chance to shift them to another public school—maybe just a few blocks away—that has better teaching or better discipline or just higher quality over all.

It's a system of self-perpetuating mediocrity: Poor schools have no incentive to improve; their students are captive clients; and parents have no opportunity to take their business elsewhere. ("Perhaps the Single Most Promising Reform Idea," 1989, p. 24)

These comments made by then President-elect George Bush in January, 1989 represent not only an endorsement but an acknowledgment of the important role choice is expected to play in America's second wave of public education reform.

While the first wave of public school reform sought improvement in student performance and teacher quality by mandating additional graduation requirements, increased testing of both students and teachers, and upgraded teacher salaries and certification, the second wave seeks improvement by changing the ways public schools are organized and controlled. Some reformers see increased choice in public education as a powerful tool for bringing about positive change in America's schools.

The term *choice* means different things to different people. As we indicated in the introduction to this book, we have chosen to focus on choice *in* public education. While a number of books have been written on school choice, most have focused on choices outside of public education (e.g., Chubb & Moe, 1990; Kearns & Doyle, 1991; Kirkpatrick, 1990; Lieberman, 1989; Rinehart & Lee, 1991). We have chosen to concentrate on the variety of choice options and plans currently in operation in public schools, districts, and states around the country.

Choice in public education is gaining political support not only from Republicans like President Bush but from Democrats as well. While President Bush has amended his 1989 call for public school choice to include vouchers for private and parochial schools, Democratic governors such as Bill Clinton of Arkansas and Booth Gardner of Washington have remained strong proponents of expanding choice within their states' public education system. Both have successfully enacted statewide choice legislation in their states. The National Governors' Association endorsed public school choice in its report, *Time for Results*, when it enthusiastically declared:

> There is nothing more basic to education and its ability to bring our children into the 21st century than choice. Given a choice in public education, we believe parents will play a stronger role in our schools. Innovative programs will spring to life. Parents and the whole community will become deeply involved in helping all children learn. Teachers will be more challenged than ever. And, most importantly, our students will see immediate results. (1986, p. 83)

The ability of choice in public education to attract support from politicians of both major parties indicates the concept has broad ideological appeal. In addition to politicians, a number of business leaders and a substantial portion of the general public support increased choice in public education. The Metropolitan Affairs Council of Detroit, the California Business Roundtable, and the Minnesota Business Partnership have all expressed support for public school choice. At the national level, the Committee for Economic Development has endorsed increased choice in public education. In the words of the Committee:

> We believe that certain market incentives and disincentives can and should be introduced into public schooling. For example, regional or even state-wide open-enrollment systems would make it possible for children and their families to choose from among a wide variety of public schools. Such freedom of choice would reward schools that met the educational objectives . . . and send a message

to those schools that are bypassed. (Research and Policy Committee, 1988, p. 28)

A poll of Wisconsin residents by the Wisconsin Policy Research
Institute in 1988 found that 75 percent of respondents believed that
parents should have the right to choose a school or district for their
children ("Across the Nation," 1988). The Minnesota Public Attitude
Survey conducted by the Minnesota Business Partnership in 1989
found 63 percent of the state's residents favored public school choice
("Public Opinion on Choice," 1989). In *The 23rd Annual Gallup Poll of
the Public's Attitudes Toward the Public Schools*, 62 percent of respondents
answered yes to the question: "Do you think that parents in this
community should or should not have the right to choose which local
schools their children attend?" Sixty percent of respondents favored
"allowing students and their parents to choose which public schools
in this community the students attend regardless of where they live"
(Elam, Rose, & Gallup, 1991, p. 47).

While choice in public education has attracted support among
politicians, business leaders, and the general public, the concept has
been less well received by public school professionals. Polls of public
school teachers and administrators reveal mixed support for choice.
A 1989 survey by the National Center for Educational Information
found that 51 percent of school board presidents, 60 percent of
principals, and 68 percent of superintendents opposed school choice
(Jennings, 1989). A 1990 survey of public school superintendents in
Washington State revealed that while 71 percent supported choice
within school districts, only 21 percent supported statewide choice
(McPherson, 1990). A 1988 poll of the Minnesota Education Association (MEA) indicated 60 percent of its membership supported statewide choice (Nathan, 1989a). Yet, the MEA opposed Minnesota's
statewide choice plan.

Concerns over teacher rights, desegregation, enrollment imbal-
ances, unhealthy competition, and an inadequate research base have
led such organizations as the National Education Association (NEA),
the American Federation of Teachers (AFT), the National Association of Elementary School Principals (NAESP), the National Association of Secondary School Principals (NASSP), and the Association
for Supervision and Curriculum Development (ASCD) to express
caution about, and in some cases, opposition to public school choice.

In 1989 the NEA passed a resolution opposing choice, which
read, in part: "The National Education Association believes that pa-

rental option or choice plans compromise the Association's commitment to free, equitable, universal, and quality public education for every student" ("Choice Spurs Debate," 1989, p. 4).

According to Scott Thomson, former Executive Director of the National Association of Secondary School Principals: "Viewed broadly . . . choice becomes a short-term expediency rather than a long-term solution. It is more likely to increase than reduce the difference in quality among school systems" (1989, p. 24). Unsure about the consequences of school choice is Paul Heckman, chairman of the Association for Supervision and Curriculum Development (ASCD) Panel on Choice. In Heckman's words: "Choice needs much more study before it becomes a policy everyone should embrace" (quoted in Rothman, 1990, p. 8).

THE KINDS OF CHOICES IN PUBLIC EDUCATION

One reason for ambivalence among school professionals and others about choice in public education is that the concept embraces a number of options and plans—school, district, and statewide. Among the better known are alternative and magnet schools, "second chance" and postsecondary programs, and both intradistrict and interdistrict plans.

Alternative and Magnet Schools

The oldest choice option in public education is alternative schools. Alternative schools were introduced in the 1960s by individuals dissatisfied with the conventional education offered in public schools. They lobbied and won support for schools that offered alternatives—such as free schools, open schools, or schools without walls—to interested students within a local district. Some of the better known early alternative schools included Community High in Berkeley, California; Metro in Chicago; Murray Road in Newton, Massachusetts; Parkway in Philadelphia; and Pilot School in Cambridge, Massachusetts. By 1981 an estimated 10,000 alternative schools were providing a variety of options to some 3 million students around the country (Raywid, 1981). In recent years, alternatives designed to serve at-risk students, such as continuation schools and learning centers, have expanded dramatically and constitute the majority of options.

Magnet schools were established in the 1970s in response to

federal court decisions requiring public school desegregation. Magnets grew rapidly, in large part because they were seen as a less controversial approach to integration than court-ordered busing, and because the federal government provided financing to encourage their implementation. Some magnets feature themes or specialized programs such as performing arts, math/science, foreign languages, or careers of various kinds which can be adapted to existing schools. Other magnets offer complete comprehensive educational approaches such as Montessori, open education, fundamental, and microsociety. In either case the purpose is to attract students from a variety of ethnic and racial backgrounds to improve integration.

By 1986 the number of magnet schools had grown to over 2,500 throughout the country (Cavazos, 1989). Today magnets are found in virtually every metropolitan school district. Examples include Atlanta's Retail program at Archer High School, Boston's International and Foreign Language program at Copley Square High School, Cincinnati's Academy of Physical Education, Dade County's Academy of Travel and Tourism, Dallas' Skyline Career Development Center, East Harlem's Isaac Newton School for Science and Math, Grand Rapids' Environmental Education program, Houston's Aerodynamics Academy, New York's LaGuardia High School of Music and the Arts, Philadelphia's High School for International Affairs, St. Paul's Saturn School of Tomorrow, and Washington, DC's Benjamin Banneker Academic High School.

Alternative and magnet schools are individual schools of choice offering special curricula and resources designed to be attractive to students from a variety of backgrounds. Most alternative and magnet schools target a specific student clientele such as at-risk, gifted, multicultural, or white and minority students for desegregation purposes. Alternative and magnet schools have no neighborhood attendance boundaries and enroll students districtwide.

"Second Chance" Options

Another choice option is "second chance" options for at-risk students and others who have not had success in the traditional schools and programs within their district. This option is designed for individuals who have had trouble with grades, attendance, or discipline and need a "second chance" to succeed. Unsuccessful students are given the option of attending public schools outside their own districts, or private nonsectarian educational clinics or learning centers at state expense. California, Colorado, Minnesota, Oregon, and Washington currently provide "second chance" options for unsuccessful students. Qualifications for participation vary by state. In Minnesota individuals must be two grade levels below normal on achievement tests or a year behind in graduation requirements, or be pregnant or assessed as chemically dependent. In Colorado individuals must have dropped out of school for at least 6 months. In California, Oregon, and Washington individuals who have simply failed school qualify for the "second chance" option. In California "second chance" enrollment is limited to private nonsectarian educational clinics or learning centers.

Postsecondary Options

Postsecondary options allow high school juniors and seniors to enroll in postsecondary institutions such as vocational/technical institutes, community colleges, and/or 4-year colleges and universities and receive both high school and college credit. Qualification and the level of tuition support vary from state to state. In Arizona, Colorado, Iowa, Maine, Minnesota, Oregon, Rhode Island, and Washington the state or school district pays the student's tuition. In Utah the cost is shared by both the student and the district. In Kansas students are responsible for all tuition costs at postsecondary institutions. To qualify in Colorado students must have fulfilled their graduation requirements and in Florida maintained a certain grade point average. Students in Maine must obtain permission from their school district to participate in postsecondary options.

Intradistrict Plans

Intradistrict plans allow students to choose from among some or all of a district's schools. Three states, Colorado, Ohio, and Washington, have passed legislation mandating intradistrict choice within all school districts. Individual districts in other states have implemented a variety of intradistrict choice plans with various degrees of choice allowed.

The oldest and most frequently found intradistrict model is that of open enrollment. In this model all students are assigned initially to neighborhood schools, after which they may enroll in other district schools on a space-available basis. Irvine and Richmond, California and Worcester, Massachusetts are examples of school districts that offer open enrollment.

A newer and increasingly popular intradistrict model is "controlled" choice. In this model there are no neighborhood schools. Most or all schools become alternative or magnet schools. Attendance boundaries for individual schools are replaced by several attendance zones that contain a number of schools, or by one zone that contains all of a district's schools. Students and their parents may apply to any school within their attendance zone or districtwide depending upon the configuration. Boston, Fall River, and Lowell, Massachusetts; Little Rock, Arkansas; Seattle, Washington; and White Plains, New York are school districts that have implemented "controlled" choice within attendance zones. Cambridge, Massachusetts; East Harlem, New York; and Montclair, New Jersey are districts that allow "controlled" choice of all schools.

"Controlled" choice models do not give students and their parents complete freedom to select the school of their choice; indeed, choice is "controlled." Families must rank their school preferences, from which the district central office or individual school makes the final assignment, taking into consideration factors such as space availability and the racial and ethnic balance of the selected schools. In general, 70 percent of families receive their first preference and 90 percent their first or second preference in "controlled" choice models.

Interdistrict Plans

Interdistrict plans allow families to choose schools outside the district in which they live. Tuition costs for the transferring student are paid to the district of choice by the resident district, the state, or the student. While students have the right to transfer, districts that are at maximum enrollment cannot be forced to take additional students. If districts have openings, however, they must accept all students. Student transfers may not contribute to racial imbalance within a school district. Transportation costs from the resident district to the district of choice are usually borne by the student's family.

To date, five states have implemented interdistrict plans. They are Arkansas, Iowa, Massachusetts, Minnesota, and Nebraska. Four other states, Idaho, Ohio, Utah, and Washington, will implement interdistrict choice in 1992–93 and 1993–94. Minnesota, the first state to implement interdistrict choice, began its plan on a voluntary basis during the 1987–88 school year. In 1990–91 the plan became mandatory for all districts. Arkansas, Iowa, and Nebraska initiated their plans during the 1990–91 school year; Massachusetts initiated its plan in 1991–92. In Arkansas and Massachusetts local districts have been given the option of not participating and do not have to accept any out-of-district students. In Iowa districts that lose more than 5 percent of their students may prohibit future transfers. In Nebraska similar restrictions apply but will be gradually phased out during a 3-year implementation period. Two states, California and Colorado, have implemented limited interdistrict plans. California allows elementary-age students to attend the schools in districts where their parents work, and Colorado encourages pilot programs, with up to three districts offering interdistrict choice.

THE CASE FOR CHOICE IN PUBLIC EDUCATION

Accountability

The concept of choice in public education has experienced a rise in popularity that has been nothing short of remarkable. In the past few years it has gone from a relatively unknown idea to a series of implemented options and plans in districts and states around the country. What has given rise to the varied and strong support for school choice? Perhaps the simplest and most accurate answer is a growing public dissatisfaction with the condition of American public education.

Evidence of this dissatisfaction can be found in the public's responses to a number of national opinion polls. A *New York Times/ CBS* nationwide poll conducted in 1988 revealed that 39 percent of Americans felt public education had worsened since 1980, while 21 percent felt it had improved. A 1988 Harris Poll for *Children* magazine found 51 percent of parents would send their children to private rather than public schools if they had the means (City Club of Chicago, 1989). Parents have not been content simply to express a preference for private schools. Between 1970 and 1985 private school enrollment grew by 6 percent, while public school enrollment declined by 17 percent (cited in Nathan, 1989c).

While America's system of public higher education is the envy of the world, its system of public elementary and secondary education is not. Numerous international studies comparing the academic performance of American and foreign students have found our students wanting, especially in the subjects of math and science. Scholastic Aptitude Test (SAT) scores have declined substantially since the mid-1960s. The National Assessment of Educational Progress reports indicate our students are not progressing very well. In 1986 only 20 percent of 11th graders could write an adequate letter; only 7 percent could do math problems that required simple algebra; and only 6 percent could read serious essays and scientific material (Finn, 1989). Finally, a chronic school dropout rate of 25 percent is graphic evidence that many students are not progressing at all.

The dissatisfaction is further compounded when it is pointed out that spending for public education grew substantially during the last decade. In 1987–88 America spent $184 billion on K–12 public education. That was an increase of 34 percent from 1983, during which time enrollment increased by less than 1 percent (Allen, 1988). Since 1950 spending on public education in constant dollars has increased by a factor of four (Chubb, 1989).

Although dissatisfaction with public education can be found throughout America, the greatest disappointment is with the nation's urban school systems. As the Carnegie report, *An Imperiled Generation: Saving Urban Schools*, declared: "This nation must see the urban school crisis for what it is: a major failure of social policy, a piecemeal approach to a problem that requires a unified response" (Carnegie Foundation for the Advancement of Teaching, 1988, p. xv).

It is in the country's largest school districts that low test scores and high dropout rates have reached alarming extremes. In Boston, Chicago, Detroit, Milwaukee, New York, Philadelphia, and Washington, DC, dropout rates exceed 40 percent. In 1983 only 7 percent of high school students in Chicago scored at or above average in reading scores (Walberg, Bakalis, Bast, & Baer, 1989). In 1989, 20 percent of high school seniors in Boston could not read at the 8th-grade level (Fiske, 1990). In 1990 the grade point average of Milwaukee's 97,000 students was 1.62 or D+ (Fund, 1990).

According to *The 23rd Annual Gallup Poll of the Public's Attitudes Towards the Public Schools*, 42 percent of all respondents gave the public schools an A or B grade, but only 27 percent of inner-city dwellers gave the same grades. Equally negative were blacks, 28 percent of whom gave their local schools A or B grades (Elam, Rose, & Gallup, 1991).

Confidence in urban public education is depressingly low. Private school enrollment is substantially higher in the cities than in the country at large. Approximately 12 percent of all children attend private schools. In 1986, 23 percent of Chicago, 21 percent of Memphis, 19 percent of San Francisco, 17 percent of Los Angeles, and 14 percent of Atlanta and Seattle children attended private schools. Even more revealing were the percentages of public school teachers in those cities who sent their own children to private schools. In

Chicago 46 percent of the city's public school teachers sent their children to private schools. In Memphis it was 36 percent; in Los Angeles, 29 percent; in San Francisco, 28 percent; in Atlanta, 25 percent; and in Seattle, 23 percent (National Governors' Association, 1986).

Although much of the movement to private schools can be attributed to white resistance to racial integration of the public schools, it is not the sole reason. Among the fastest growing numbers of participants in private education are those of minority and economically disadvantaged parents. Minority enrollment in America's elementary and secondary Catholic schools increased from 11 percent in 1971 to 22 percent in 1987. Non-Catholic enrollment, the majority of which was black, increased from 3 to 12 percent during the same time (Pavuk, 1987). The choice of private education represents a substantial sacrifice for poor and minority families. The fact that increasing numbers of them are making the sacrifice indicates widespread dissatisfaction with the quality of urban public education.

Dissatisfaction with urban public education has led to an increase in support for private schools and the privatization of public schools. In Chicago several major corporations, tired of waiting for the city's school system to reform, opened their own private elementary school. In 1988 Sears Roebuck, United Airlines, Penmark International, and Baxter International opened the Corporate/Community School in Lawndale, one of Chicago's poorest neighborhoods. One thousand children applied for 150 openings in grades K–3. Eventually the Corporate/Community School will expand to serve 300 children in grades K–8. In Dade County, Florida the school board has signed a 5-year contract with Education Alternatives Inc., a forprofit company, to operate one of its elementary schools beginning September, 1992. More dramatic is the decision of the Chelsea, Massachusetts school district, which turned over its entire school system to Boston University for a 10-year period beginning in the fall of 1989.

If public schools hope to slow the movement toward private education or privatization, especially in the cities, they must change. If they fail to do so, public education will continue to lose not only the 25–40 percent of economically disadvantaged and underachieving students who drop out, but also the economically advantaged and highly motivated students who are increasingly patronizing private education.

There is a public perception that the nation's schools are not turning out competent graduates. The statistics of declining academic performance mentioned earlier are evidence for some Americans that public education is not doing its job. Although continuing adequate financial support of public education is necessary, increased funding will not, by itself, be sufficient to improve students' academic performance. Introducing options and choice is one of the keys to improving academic performance and increasing confidence in public education.

A number of research studies have found a positive relationship between the introduction of choice options and plans, and improved student academic performance. Alternative schools have had success in improving attendance and academic performance of at-risk students (Young, 1990). School districts such as East Harlem, New York; Cambridge and Lowell, Massachusetts; and Montclair, New Jersey have reported increased test scores with the implementation of magnet schools and intradistrict plans.

The introduction of choice in urban school systems can reduce the flight to private schools and increase enrollment in public schools. In the Georgetown area of Washington, DC, a magnet school complex of six schools increased public school enrollment from 11 percent of all school-age children in 1980 to 63 percent in 1987 (Jones, 1988). Prince George's County, Maryland managed to attract 3,000 students previously enrolled in private schools since instituting magnet schools in 1985. Buffalo, New York has had similar success in attracting parochial and private school students back into the public education system (Snider, 1987). A 1985 survey of Boston private school parents by the Citywide Educational Coalition asked respondents if they would return to public education if given the opportunity to select a "high-quality" public school anywhere in the district. Many said they would "very seriously" consider transferring back to the district.

Offering a variety of attractive, high-quality options and giving parents greater choice in selecting those options has the potential of generating greater satisfaction with, and participation in, public education. Families that choose the schools their children attend are more likely to be supportive of such schools than of those their children are compelled to attend. When a parent or student chooses a school, there is an emotional investment and subsequent commitment that ensure parents and students will try to make the educational experience a success. As Sy Fliegel, former school administrator from East Harlem, observed: "It's an old capitalist idea that people just treat what they own much better than things they don't" (U.S. Department of Education, 1989, p. 12).

Choice also introduces an element of competition which can promote accountability. As the National Governors' Association declared: "If we implement broader choice plans, true choice among public schools, then we unlock the values of competition in the educational marketplace. Schools that compete for students, teachers, and dollars will, by virtue of their environment, make those changes which allow them to succeed" (1986, p. 83).

Choice promotes accountability because a public school no longer has a captive clientele that can be taken for granted. Families, unhappy with the educational product they are receiving, are free to choose another school under intradistrict plans, or another district under interdistrict plans.

Public schools of choice compete for students. Thus they must have something to offer families if they hope to attract enough students to receive adequate funding. Fear of a student exodus can be a powerful incentive for a district, or a school within a district, to make changes and improve, because declining enrollment means the loss of state monies and ultimately of teaching and administrative positions. When schools have to appeal to parents and students, they pay more attention to quality and accept greater responsibility for the educational outcomes they produce.

Competition is not without its drawbacks, however. Public education is not a private commodity but a public good. Public schools must serve all students whether they are above or below average in ability, handicapped, at risk, or bilingual. Choice options and plans of equal educational quality must be available for all students.

Choice options and plans must recognize that all families do not possess the same degree of knowledge and sophistication about the schools and programs available to their children. Nor do families have the same amount of free time or financial resources to inquire about and participate in special options and plans. Public school choice must be well conceived and carefully implemented to avoid pitting families against one another in unhealthy or unfair ways. Choice must promote equity as well as accountability.

Equity

It is no secret that public schools have not provided all members of our society with a quality education. Minority and low-income children, in particular, have suffered from unequal educational opportunities. As the National Coalition of Advocates for Children observed:

> Minority children do not matter as much as non-minority children, judging by the disproportionate numbers of such children who are excluded and underserved by the schools. We know, for example, that black students are placed in classes for the mildly mentally handicapped at rates more than three times that of white children. Poor children, too, are considered less important than non-poor children, if we contrast the level of financing allocated for their education with that allocated for children in more affluent districts. (1985, pp. *viii–ix*)

Affluent parents have a variety of choices available to them by virtue of their wealth. They may choose to live in a community with a reputation for an excellent public school system, or they may choose to live in a community for other reasons and send their children to private schools. Poor parents do not have such choices. As Joan Ratteray, president of the Institute for Independent Education, observed: "Most Black Americans have only one 'choice': inner city schools that have become the dregs of the nation's educational system" (quoted in City Club of Chicago, 1989, p. 8).

Even when public school systems implement desegregation plans, minority students have not always reaped the benefits. Most desegregation plans have used neighborhood-based remedies such as redrawing school attendance boundaries. Boundaries, particularly those for elementary schools, are usually not large enough to incorporate a mixed-race population. Attendance boundaries are also vulnerable to population shifts within a city. Desegregation plans in Dallas, Texas; Mobile, Alabama; and Pasadena, California left between 40 and 60 percent of black pupils in nearly all-black schools (Alves & Willie, 1987).

Intradistrict plans, like "controlled" choice, increase educational opportunities and equity for economically disadvantaged or minority families by allowing them to select from among many or all of a district's schools. School assignment is not dependent upon neighborhood housing patterns. All students, advantaged and disadvantaged, majority and minority, have equal or proportional access to all schools and programs of choice.

Interdistrict plans have the potential of giving families even greater educational opportunity and equity. Families, dissatisfied with the quality of education within their own school district, are given the choice of sending their children to schools in other districts. Interdistrict plans increase equity by offering minority and low-income students an education heretofore reserved for suburban white and middle-class Americans.

Today, more than 60 percent of mothers with school-age children work full time. One in two marriages ends in divorce. Thirty percent of all children have no adult at home when they return from school. With fewer adults in the home as a result of these changes, children are increasingly experiencing an erosion of social capital. According to James Coleman, social capital is "the range of exchange between parents and children about academic, social, economic, and personal matters" (1987, p. 37). Parents are increasingly turning to public and private institutions to provide the missing social capital for their children.

While all children have been affected by the movement of adults out of the home and decreasing participation in childrearing, the trend has been most harmful to disadvantaged children. Advantaged parents are able to enroll their children in private schools and programs that provide the missing social capital and character formation on behalf of absent parents. Poor parents, on the other hand, do not have the economic resources to compensate for their increasing absence from the home. As a result, parents who cannot afford private options are increasingly asking schools to provide the missing social capital in their children's lives. Choice allows the development of such schools and programs. As David Kearns and Dennis Doyle note, meeting the needs of disadvantaged children is a major reason for embracing schools of choice.

> One aspect of choice systems that deserves special note is the beneficial impact it could have on the underclass. . . . The single most important resource these people need is access to schools that serve their needs. By that we mean not only schools that offer a full array of ancillary services, such as health clinics and day care, but schools that are community-based, schools that can expect to modify the social as well as academic behavior of students. (1991, pp. 36–37)

Public alternative schools, designed to serve at-risk students, can take on the role of social agency as well as that of educational institution by offering a variety of social–psychological services such as counseling, drug and alcohol rehabilitation, work and independent study credits, and flexible scheduling. Many such schools provide day care facilities to serve students who have children. In addition, some schools have gone to extended day and year schedules to meet better the needs of students and parents.

The variety and quality of the social–psychological services provided become the measures by which some parents and community members evaluate their schools. For some, educational excellence is not defined simply in terms of intellectual rigor or academic comprehensiveness but in terms of meeting a variety of economic, social, and psychological needs. It is doubtful whether public education, as traditionally conceived, can successfully deliver what at-risk students need. Increased options and choice can promote a variety of compensatory services, a diversity of curricular and instructional approaches, and a broader definition of educational excellence.

Diversity

It is well known that individual students have different needs, interests, abilities, and ways of learning. Different curricula, instructional approaches, even teacher personalities can affect student learning. Some students benefit from a "back-to-basics" approach, while others learn best in open-education, continuous-progress, cooperative-learning, or individualized approaches to instruction. In addition, teachers can be more or less effective teaching with different techniques and with different kinds of students. Choice allows teachers, as well as students, to select the school or program that best fits their instructional or learning style.

Although the expanded-care, extended-year school mentioned earlier may be an effective model for some students and their families, it is not appropriate for everyone. Many students neither need nor want social–psychological services. Parents who are able or willing to provide the necessary social capital for their children would find an expanded-care, extended-year school an unnecessary duplication of the services provided at home. All students do not need, nor are they well served by attending, the same kind of school. As Mary Anne Raywid has observed:

> Today's schools serve youngsters whose backgrounds, interests, hopes, and talents vary widely. Not all of them will thrive under the single set of conditions we have laid down for our schools. To

succeed, they will need different kinds of school environments, different kinds of instructional approaches, and differently packaged content. (1987, p. 766)

Raywid's observation is not a new one. Similar observations were made almost 20 years ago in such studies as *Youth: Transition to Adulthood* (1974) and *The Education of Adolescents* (1976). Both recognized the inadequacy of a single school model and recommended the formation of differentiated or theme schools which would offer choices among such specializations as music, physical education, science, arts, and so forth. The studies advocated restructuring schools to include minischools, schools within schools, schools without walls, and open schools. The studies also recommended more integration of school and work by allowing students to spend part of the day involved in apprentice and action learning in work settings outside the school.

More recently, the Carnegie Council report, *Turning Points: Preparing American Youth for the 21st Century* (1989), made similar recommendations and called for increased diversity and choice in public education. The authors of that report advocated flexibility in organization of the school day, reorganization of school structures, differentiated staffing, and varied instructional approaches.

Choice in public education allows schools to diversify and concentrate their resources and energy in a limited number of areas, thus maximizing their effectiveness. As mentioned earlier, alternative and magnet schools offer programs that are designed for a specific clientele (e.g., at-risk, gifted, multicultural) and offer a specialized program of study (e.g., vocational, humanities, science/math, performing arts). The narrow focus of these schools allows them to concentrate on what they do best rather than try to be all things to all students. The ability to specialize and provide a focused educational program is a distinctive feature and strength of alternative and magnet schools. As the National Governors' Association recognized in its 1986 report, *Time for Results*:

> Experience with public alternative schools shows that many have the distinct shared philosophy, mission, and faculty agreement called for in the literature on effective schools. Indeed, many outstanding schools share certain characteristics of effective corporations. One of the similarities is clear, distinct, focused mission. When schools are permitted to develop some specialization, their effectiveness increases. (p. 69)

Schools that serve a specific clientele or specialize in a certain program have greater agreement among staff and students about the philosophy and direction of the school. Participants share a common core of values and have a clear vision of what the school is about. This common core of values provides greater opportunity for meeting both individual and group needs and avoiding alienation among individual members. As Fred Newmann observes, public schools of choice can reduce student and parent alienation because ". . . students and their parents voluntarily develop and attend schools whose purposes they share" (1989, p. 159).

The conventional public school model, which serves a heterogeneous student clientele, cannot concentrate its resources and efforts on any particular group of students without alienating other groups. The typical response, therefore, is to offer a standardized program that does not offend but pleases no one. The result of this standardization, according to David Kearns and Dennis Doyle, is that "public elementary and secondary schools sink to the lowest common denominator. Because they must be all things to all people, they lose their identity, their autonomy, and eventually their integrity" (1991, p. 29).

The reluctance to give up the conventional model of the public school is due, in large part, to the misconception that sameness means equality and that differences mean inequality. As Gerald Grant reminds us, however, such reasoning is faulty:

> The laudable effort to overcome harmful inequalities has led to the presumption that all differences between schools must be extinguished on the grounds that they reflect inequalities. . . .
>
> Tolstoy was wrong when he wrote that "all happy families are like one another." They are alike in that they are happy, but the kinds and qualities of happiness and the forms and activities through which it is achieved are many. If each slavishly followed a plan for happy families developed by the ministry, they might be more alike but fewer would be happy. So it is with schools. (1988, p. 222)

While educational differences can lead to inequalities, they do not have to do so. When properly designed and implemented, choice options and plans can offer a variety of *quality* schools and programs that serve the needs of *all* students. Such an approach works not only in affluent suburban districts but in less advantaged urban districts as well. The East Harlem, New York school district serves a population that is predominantly poor and minority. Yet it has developed an intradistrict plan that has gained considerable publicity and praise around the country. The rationale behind East Harlem's plan is diversity for every student. As former deputy superintendent Sy Fliegel explains:

> The aim here has been to create a system that—instead of trying to fit students into some standardized school—has a school to fit every student in this district. No one gets left out; no one gets lost. Every kid is important; *every* kid can learn if you put him into the right environment. But since kids have this huge range of different needs, different interests, and different ways of learning we've got to have a wide diversity of schools. (quoted in Clinchy, 1989, p. 291; emphasis in original)

In East Harlem all junior high schools are individual schools of choice. Students and their families must select from among 23 different alternative schools. Each offers a theme with curriculum organized around it; some of the themes are math, maritime careers, performing arts, science, communications, environmental science, and health services. However they may differ in other ways, each school offers a quality program, and all 23 schools have at one time or another been cited as exemplary.

Choice in public education forces us to abandon the false notion that there should or can be a single, all-inclusive definition of educational excellence, a single standardized approach to schooling, a single way of organizing and operating a school that is suitable for all students and serves all students equally well. Choice creates different kinds of schools to serve our diverse student population and to accommodate the range of parent and professional beliefs about what public education should be.

SUMMARY

We have argued in this chapter that the introduction of choice in public education has the potential for promoting greater educational accountability, equity, and diversity. We believe choice holds the key to improving public education by increasing parent, student, and teacher participation and by broadening the definition of excellence to meet the wide range of talents, interests, and needs of *all* students. We have also cautioned that choice brings with it increased risks as well as benefits. Finally, we have observed that the concept of choice embraces a variety of options and plans such as alternative and magnet schools, "second chance" and postsecondary options, intradistrict and interdistrict plans.

Our discussion of choice has been general, with little empirical evidence to support the concept in practice. Parents and school professionals interested in choice in public education want more than generalities, however. They want empirical data that will help them answer specific questions about the benefits and risks of public school choice, questions like: Do all students or only a few benefit from choice? How much will choice cost? Which choice options or plans are most effective in promoting greater educational accountability, equity, and diversity? In Chapter 2 we will attempt to answer these questions by analyzing the research on choice.

CHAPTER TWO

How Effective Is Choice
in Public Education?

In Chapter 1 we learned that choice in public education embraces a number of options and plans such as alternative and magnet schools, "second chance" and postsecondary options, intradistrict and interdistrict plans. In this chapter we review research on each of the choice options and plans to determine its effectiveness. The criteria for effectiveness is how well the option or plan promotes educational accountability, equity, and diversity.

Two limitations regarding this review need to be mentioned. First, all of the choice options and plans have not been studied equally. While numerous studies have analyzed alternative and magnet schools and intradistrict plans, little research has been conducted on "second chance" and postsecondary programs, and interdistrict plans. The disparity in the quantity and quality of research means that conclusions about the effectiveness of each choice option or plan cannot be made with the same level or degree of confidence. Second, most of the research is correlational. Although correlational studies can demonstrate that relationships or associations among variables exist, they do not allow us to draw conclusions about cause and effect. With these two limitations in mind, let us begin the review.

ALTERNATIVE AND MAGNET SCHOOLS

Alternative and magnet schools are individual schools of choice that feature themes or specialized programs such as back-to-basics, performing arts, math/science, foreign languages, career education; or offer complete comprehensive educational approaches such as Montessori, fundamental, open education, microsociety, and so forth. In either case, alternative and magnet schools are usually designed to attract specific groups of students such as at-risk, gifted, vocational, or multiethnic and multiracial for desegregation purposes.

Research on alternative schools has not been as extensive as research on magnet schools. Research on the former has focused primarily upon schools that serve at-risk students. A 1984 study by Martin Gold and David Mann compared 60 at-risk students from three alternative secondary schools with a matched group of students from conventional secondary schools in the same districts. Results indicated:

1. By the end of the year, alternative students were less disruptive in school than conventional students.
2. Teachers rated alternative students who returned to conventional schools as better behaved than conventional students.
3. Alternative students were more positive about school than were their conventional counterparts.
4. Alternative students received improved grades when they reenrolled in conventional schools.

Two studies by Eileen Foley, one with Susan McConnaughy in 1982 and one with Peggy Crull in 1984, followed the progress of 300 at-risk students attending eight alternative high schools. Results indicated that after 2 years alternative programs had cut student absences by 40 percent, increased credits earned by more than 60 percent, but had not significantly improved graduation rates.

A positive relationship between alternative education and improved attendance was found by Mary Ann Raywid in her 1982 survey of 1,200 secondary alternative schools and programs. Eighty-one percent of the schools reported student attendance had increased compared to patterns at previous schools.

The relationship of student and teacher attitudes in seven alternative and six conventional schools was analyzed by Gerald Smith, Thomas Gregory, and Richard Pugh in 1981. The authors found that both alternative students and teachers scored higher than their conventional counterparts in having their social, esteem, security, and self-actualization needs met. Similar results were reported by Gregory and Smith in a 1987 study that compared a small alternative high school with a large conventional high school.

Larger scale and more rigorous studies have analyzed the effectiveness of magnet schools. A U.S. Department of Education Study undertaken by Patricia Fleming and others in 1982 examined more than 1,000 magnet schools and found them to have fewer student behavior problems and higher teacher satisfaction than conventional public schools. Researchers also found greater teacher and student commitment in magnets than in conventional schools.

A more detailed study of 45 magnets in 15 urban districts by Rolf Blank and others in 1983 concluded that magnet schools provided high-quality education. One third of the schools were rated high in every category and more than half were rated high in most categories as identified by the researchers. The categories included "(1) having a special curricular theme or method of instruction, (2) playing a unique role in desegregation within its district, (3) relying on voluntary enrollment, and (4) offering open access to students beyond a regular attendance zone" (1984, pp. 270–271). Magnet schools were also successful in promoting high student achievement. Eighty percent of magnet students had achievement scores in reading and math that were above the average for their respective districts.

A 1985 study of 41 magnet schools in eight school districts was conducted by the New York State Education Department. It found that magnet schools significantly improved student achievement and attendance, and lowered dropout rates. A majority of the 41 schools had achievement scores that were higher than their district averages. Ninety-eight percent of the magnets had higher attendance, and three fourths had lower dropout rates than their district averages.

A series of studies conducted by the Los Angeles Unified School District from 1983–86 in 84 magnet schools found students' reading and math scores to be above district averages. In addition, researchers found that the longer students attended the magnet programs, the greater their relative advantage. Finally, students in magnet schools displayed greater on task behavior, and manifested more positive attitudes about school than students in nonmagnet schools (cited in Raywid, 1989).

A 1988 study by John Larsen and Brenda Allen of 14 magnet schools in Montgomery County, Maryland found results similar to those of Los Angeles. Students' reading and math scores in magnet schools were above district averages, and the longer students remained in magnet schools, the greater their advantage grew over their conventional counterparts. Even less successful students had positive attitudes about their magnet school.

In 1976 Montclair, New Jersey instituted a districtwide magnet school program. An evaluation of the program by Educational Testing Service (ETS) found improved test scores in reading and math for both black and white students between 1974 and 1986. In reading, the percentage of black students below grade level declined from 57 to 43 percent during those years, and for white students from 22 to 14 percent. In math, the percentage of black students below grade level declined from 62 to 36 percent, and for whites from 28 to 8 percent (Clewell & Joy, 1990).

In 1984, 3rd graders in Prince George's County, Maryland scored at the 58th percentile on the California Achievement Test. In 1985 the district instituted magnet programs in 44 of the district's 175 schools. By 1987, 3rd-grade scores had risen to the 73rd percentile. Similar gains occurred for 5th and 8th graders. In addition, the gap between white and black students also narrowed during this time (Steinbach & Pierce, 1989).

Mary Metz's year-long study of three magnet schools within the same district concluded that magnets helped to improve academic performance for less advantaged students. Innovations in the magnet schools made it easier to work with students from diverse backgrounds and with those who had academic and social difficulties. According to Metz, "The magnet schools could and did serve the less privileged children of the city well" (1986, p. 210).

The success of magnet schools has led observers like Dennis Doyle and Marsha Levine to conclude that neighborhood schools no longer make sense. They see magnet schools, particularly in urban areas, as powerful tools for educational change. "Magnet schools offer a strategy for low-cost, highly visible, incremental change that could conceivably transform American education" (1984, p. 270).

While magnets are an effective choice option, they are not without their drawbacks. Despite the claim of Doyle and Levine, magnets are rarely low-cost options. Magnets typically cost 10 to 12 percent more to operate than nonmagnet schools and programs, although the percentage usually declines the longer the magnet is in operation (Snider, 1987). Some magnets can be even more expensive. During 1986–87, St. Louis spent 25 to 42 percent more on magnet students than on nonmagnet students (Nathan, 1989c). East Harlem, which operates a nationally recognized intradistrict plan that utilizes junior high school alternative programs, was at one point receiving more federal funding per student than any other school district in the country (Snider, 1989).

Aside from their increased cost, magnets have had limited success in promoting racial and ethnic desegregation. In Los Angeles, where 26,000 students attended 86 magnet schools in 1988–89, seats for Anglo students went unfilled in inner-city magnets while magnets in Anglo areas were swamped with requests. In 1987–88 St. Louis provided transportation to encourage transfers between its district and 16 suburban districts. Some 11,000 black students took advantage of the plan and enrolled in suburban schools. However, only 626 suburban white students chose to attend one of the 26 magnet schools in St. Louis (Nathan, 1989c). In fact, 9 of the 12 magnet schools in St. Louis had vacancies but had to turn away black students because of low enrollment percentages among whites (Snider, 1987).

Districts that have had some success in school desegregation through magnet programs, such as Buffalo, New York; Milwaukee, Wisconsin; and Prince George's County, Maryland have found that magnets alone are not the answer. Milwaukee and Buffalo magnetized considerable numbers of their schools but still had substantial numbers of students attending all-minority and near-all-minority schools. According to Larry Hughes, William Gordon, and Larry Hillman, there has been "no instance where a major school system has achieved noticeable desegregation in its public schools by using a voluntary magnet program" (1980, p. 20).

One reason for magnets' limited success in promoting desegregation is that there usually are not enough of them to go around. While virtually every large school district in America offers some form of magnet school or program, very few have converted all of their schools and programs into magnets. As a result, most students within a district are not able to take advantage of them.

Furthermore, some magnets use selection criteria such as grades, tests, and grade point averages for admittance, so every student may not qualify for a magnet school or program. Approximately one third of magnets have admission requirements such as test scores and grades, making it difficult for less academically qualified students to gain admittance to selective schools and programs (Blank, 1984). It is no wonder, then, that magnet students outperform their conventional counterparts. The surprise would be if they did not.

A 1988 study by Donald Moore and Suzanne Davenport drew attention to some of the negative consequences of implementing magnet schools and programs. Moore and Davenport examined magnets in the school districts of Boston, Chicago, New York City, and Philadelphia and found that these schools favored students with good academic, attendance, and behavior records at the expense of those with learning problems. Complex application procedures discouraged less sophisticated and motivated parents from signing their children up for magnets. Transfer practices returned undesirable students to their neighborhood schools and contributed to the disparity between neighborhood and magnet schools. Competition for students who were already performing well reduced district interest in improving education for all students. According to Moore and Davenport, "A system that is supposed to provide students with choices has, too frequently, left the typical entering high school student in our big cities, and especially students at risk, out in the cold" (1989, p. 7).

Similar observations about inadequate information and unequal participation in magnet programs have been made by other researchers. Susan Uchitelle (1978) found that minority and low-income parents in a midwestern school district were not as knowledgeable about the opportunities for choice as were their middle- and upper-income counterparts. Robert Arnove and Toby Strout (1978) found different levels of quality among alternative schools. Arnove and Strout concentrated on options specifically designed and reserved for disadvantaged or at-risk students and found these programs were used primarily to remove and isolate such students from mainstream schools and programs. Undesirable students were "dumped" into remedial programs, in which the numbers of poor and minority students were disproportionately high.

To reduce inequities alternative or magnet schools may engender, Moore and Davenport offer several recommendations including a centralized selection process to ensure consistent and fair admission criteria are being applied, program selection based on student interest not performance, careful monitoring of information dissemination and student counseling to ensure biases are not introduced, and equitable funding of all schools and programs.

Joe Nathan (1988) has suggested a number of conditions to be met before introducing alternative or magnet schools or other choice options or plans within a school district:

1. Free transportation should be provided to facilitate participation by all families.
2. Implementation of racial balance procedures must be undertaken to ensure assignments do not discriminate against students.
3. School and program selection cannot be based on a first-come, first-served principle.
4. A wide range of programs at many, if not all, schools should be offered rather than a limited number of programs at a few selected schools.
5. Adequate provision of information and counseling to parents must be made to facilitate informed parental selection.

6. Alternative, magnets and other choice options and plans should avoid selective criteria for participation. Student interest should be the criterion for participation.

Nathan's preconditions go a long way in answering the objections of Moore and Davenport. Provision of adequate information and counseling regarding available options and plans, as well as free transportation, ensure greater participation by all families interested in choice. The elimination of selective criteria and the implementation of racial and ethnic balance procedures discourage options and plans from becoming elitist and siphoning off the better students.

Perhaps the most important of Nathan's recommendations is the expansion of alternative and magnet schools and programs. While increased information, free transportation, elimination of admission criteria, and adoption of racial and ethnic balance procedures may reduce some of the inequities, implementation of those recommendations will do nothing to solve the problem of a limited number of special schools or programs that serve only a percentage of students. To resolve this problem districts need to expand alternative and magnet schools and programs.

Introducing a variety of thematic or specialized programs from which all students may choose promotes equity and diversity. More alternative and magnet schools mean a more equitable distribution of education monies throughout a district because financing is not concentrated upon a few special programs or schools. The best approach is to make all district schools alternatives or magnets and allow students to choose the school or program they prefer. Access to the school must not be limited by admission requirements, inadequate dissemination of information, or lack of transportation. If access is limited, then the equity and diversity gained through the introduction of alternatives and magnets would be lost. If implemented properly, alternative and magnet schools and programs have the potential to promote accountability, equity, and diversity in public education.

INTRADISTRICT CHOICE PLANS

Alum Rock Public Voucher Demonstration Project

An early intradistrict plan was an open enrollment experiment conducted by the federal government in the early 1970s. In 1972 the

Office of Economic Opportunity funded a Voucher Demonstration Project in Alum Rock Union Elementary School District in San Jose, California. In 1973 the National Institute of Education assumed sponsorship of the project until its termination in 1977. Parents were given vouchers that were used to select any public school within the district. Schools, in turn, exchanged the vouchers for cash. To attract students schools established a number of special alternative minischools and programs. Families that did not want to participate in the voucher experiment had the option of sending their children to their neighborhood schools.

A 3-year study of the project was published by the Rand Corporation in 1981. Results of that study included the following:

1. At the school level, reading scores of students whose parents had chosen special alternative minischools and programs were not appreciably different from those of students in regular programs.
2. At the classroom level, reading achievement was higher in classrooms where teachers saw themselves as autonomous.
3. Teacher perceptions of their autonomy and of their alternative program affected students' reading achievement.
4. Significant differences existed in family awareness of school and program choices. Initially, economically advantaged families had more and better information from which to make choices than did economically disadvantaged families. Over time, however, differences between families diminished as parents gained experience in making choices.
5. Economically advantaged and disadvantaged parents made different choices for their children. Advantaged parents typically chose open, less structured classrooms for their children, while disadvantaged parents chose more structured, traditional classrooms.
6. The intradistrict plan resulted in slightly better districtwide racial balance.

Results from the Alum Rock Public Demonstration Project are mixed. Schoolwide achievement did not improve significantly, but there was some improvement at the classroom level. In terms of equity, district racial balance improved slightly, but economically advantaged and disadvantaged families segregated themselves by the programs and schools they selected. The quantity and quality of information possessed by families to make choices also differed along socioeconomic lines, although the differences diminished over time. The intradistrict plan improved the distribution of district resources among all schools. Instead of a few special schools and programs receiving extra district monies, all district schools and programs were treated equally and received the same financial support. Finally, the most positive feature of the Alum Rock Demonstration Project was increased diversity through the conversion of all schools into "alternative" schools and programs of choice.

East Harlem, New York

One of the best-known intradistrict plans is that of East Harlem, New York. East Harlem school district serves some 14,300 largely bilingual, minority, and economically disadvantaged students. Historically, East Harlem had been the worst performing district among the 32 community school districts in New York City (Domanico, 1989).

In 1974 the district introduced three alternative programs designed to attract junior high students from around the district. Three more were created in 1975, two each in 1976, 1978, 1979, 1980, and three more in 1981. In 1982 five more alternative programs were instituted, along with an intradistrict plan that required all parents to choose which junior high school or program they wanted their child to attend. Since 1982 all 23 junior highs have been alternative schools or programs. The alternatives include such thematic programs as performing arts, careers, sports, science, humanities, health, maritime, environmental sciences, and the nationally recognized Central Park East Secondary School. Parents indicate their preferences from first to third, and the individual alternative schools make the final determination. Typically, 60 percent of parents get their first choice, 30 percent their second, and 5 percent their third. The remaining 5 percent are placed at district discretion after consultation with parents (Domanico, 1989).

Prior to the combination of alternative schools with an intradistrict plan, East Harlem performed at the bottom of the 32 community school districts in New York City. By 1989 it was 16th out of the 32 districts. In 1974 only 15 percent of East Harlem students were at or above grade level in reading; in 1988, 62 percent were. Since 1983, when citywide math testing was instituted, test scores of East Harlem students have been virtually unchanged, but the district's position has gone from 23rd to 19th out of the 32 community school districts (Domanico, 1989). East Harlem's success has prompted out-of-district students, including white children, to seek admission to its schools. In addition to improved test scores, East

Harlem has been successful in getting its students into New York City's selective public high schools. In 1987, 23 percent of East Harlem's junior high graduates were admitted to top city selective public high schools, while the average for all community school districts was only 9 percent.

Although its intradistrict plan has helped to make East Harlem an effective school district, it is not the sole reason for that effectiveness. Curricular reforms, smaller schools, and increased funding have also contributed to East Harlem's success. In addition to these reforms, the influx of out-of-district students has contributed to the improvement in East Harlem's test scores. Many out-of-district students come from more advantaged neighborhoods and are above-average students. While individual schools are not supposed to enroll more than 20 percent of out-of-district students, some admit more (Snider, 1989).

In addition to admitting out-of-district students, individual schools are allowed to set their own admission criteria and make their own student selections. These practices raise equity concerns because advantaged out-of-district students sometimes gain admittance to the more selective schools at the expense of less advantaged in-district students. According to some East Harlem teachers, "most local students have virtually no chance of attending the district's 'elite' public schools which accept only students with reading scores in the highest percentiles" (quoted in Snider, 1989, p. 13).

District officials respond to this criticism by maintaining that student needs can be met better, and an effective match between school and student can be made, when schools have the prerogative to set criteria and select their student body. As John Falco, director of the district's magnet program, points out: "If a student reading at the 13th percentile wants to attend a school where most of the students are reading above the 75th percentile, could I in all good conscience place that child in that setting?" (quoted in Snider, 1989, p. 13).

As Moore and Davenport (1989), Arnove and Strout (1978), and Uchitelle (1978) found from their respective studies, choice programs with admission criteria lead to inequities. Average or below-average students or students of poorly informed parents are frequently at a disadvantage in competitive choice options and plans. East Harlem's practice of allowing individual schools to set admission criteria and select students aggravates, rather than reduces, such inequities.

The primary strength of East Harlem's intradistrict plan has been its positive relationship with improved academic achievement.

The conversion of all the district's junior high schools into alternative schools and programs provides greater educational opportunities for students and thus promotes diversity. The primary weakness of East Harlem's intradistrict plan remains its practice of allowing individual schools to set admission criteria and select their own students.

Cambridge, Massachusetts

Another well-known success story is Cambridge, Massachusetts. Located next to Boston, Cambridge is a compact school district of 6.2 square miles serving some 7,500 students. The district is a combination of lower-middle-class and upper-middle-class families, the latter largely employed by Harvard or the Massachusetts Institute of Technology. Approximately 50 percent of the district is minority in composition and contains some 46 different language groups.

In 1981 a "controlled" choice intradistrict plan was implemented as part of a desegregation effort begun 2 years earlier. As a result of the plan, families may choose from among all of the district's 13 K–8 elementary schools. The district's one high school is attended by all students. The 13 elementary schools offer a variety of alternative programs which include language immersion, writing across the curriculum, future studies, gifted and talented, whole language, computer assisted instruction, and so forth.

Unlike families in East Harlem, Cambridge families do not apply directly to individual schools. Parents must submit their school preferences to a central Parent Information Center (PIC), which is responsible for the final placement of all students. Racial balance is the first and most important criterion for school assignment. No school may enroll more than 55 percent minority or majority students. Other criteria include student distance from a school (closer students have preference) and school assignment of siblings (students with siblings in a school have preference). The "controlled" choice approach to school assignment works well. Typically, 90 percent of all students receive their first choice and 5 percent their second choice. Five percent are assigned at the discretion of the district.

In Cambridge individual schools may not set selective criteria for student enrollment. There are no admission requirements for any of the district's 13 schools. Schools are selected on the basis of parent and student interest. All programs are available to every student, although families must provide their own transportation.

Improved student performance is associated with Cambridge's intradistrict "controlled" choice plan. In 1984–85, 79 percent of all students passed the California Test of Basic Skills in math, 76 percent passed in reading, and 59 percent passed writing. Overall, 54 percent of the students passed in all three areas. In 1987–88, 88 percent passed in math, 84 percent in reading, and 91 percent in writing. Overall, 87 percent passed in all three areas. Further evidence of improvement was an increase in the percentage of public school enrollment among school age children. Seventy-eight percent of Cambridge's kindergarten students attended public schools in 1978; in 1987, 89 percent did. During that time, the percentage of public school enrollment at all grade levels increased from 80 to 85 percent (Peterkin & Jones, 1989). As with East Harlem, however, choice has not been the sole reason for improved academic performance and increased public support. Adequate funding, curricular reform, and small school size have also contributed to Cambridge's success. In addition, the district's ability to attract students from private schools has probably helped to increase districtwide test scores.

Not only has student academic performance improved but ethnic and racial desegregation as well. All 13 of the district's schools are within 10 percentage points plus or minus of the districtwide averages for race and ethnicity. What is noteworthy about Cambridge's success is that increased accountability has not come at the price of unequal student participation. The centralized approach to school assignment and the absence of school admission criteria have promoted equity in student participation.

Of the three intradistrict plans reviewed here, the "controlled" choice model appears to hold the most promise for promoting accountability, equity, and diversity. Cambridge's centralized school assignment procedure and elimination of school admission criteria improve upon East Harlem's intradistrict plan by ensuring that all students have an equal or proportional chance to enroll in the school of their choice. The only additional improvement Cambridge might make to enhance equity further would be to provide free transportation to all of its schools. Fortunately, the city's compact size and abundance of public transportation make it relatively convenient for students to attend any of the district's 13 schools.

Adoption of either East Harlem's or Cambridge's intradistrict plan does not come cheaply, however. At one point, as mentioned earlier in this chapter, East Harlem had the highest per pupil expenditure of any school district in America. Cambridge has received substantial state and federal funding for its desegregation efforts. A number of other school districts have implemented their own intra-district "controlled" choice plans. Among the more successful are Lowell, Massachusetts and Montclair, New Jersey.

"SECOND CHANCE" OPTIONS

"Second chance" options allow unsuccessful students to attend public schools outside of their district and in some cases attend private educational clinics or learning centers at state expense. In 1985 Colorado passed the Education Quality Act which, among other things, established "second chance" programs for students aged 16–21 who had dropped out of school for 6 months or more. Regional "second chance" centers were established to provide course work towards high school diplomas and general equivalency diplomas (GED). In 1986 four centers were serving 170 students. By 1990, 14 centers had been established and over 1,000 students were enrolled. A survey conducted during the 1988–89 school year indicated 959 students had enrolled in "second chance" centers. Of those, 219 had received their diploma and 81 their GED (Colorado Department of Education, 1990).

Washington State allows students aged 13–19 who have dropped out, been suspended for a month or more, or expelled to enroll at state expense in private educational clinics. An evaluation of that program in 1985 by a budget committee of the state legislature concluded that over half of the approximately 1,100 students attending educational clinics were motivated to achieve and engaged in constructive activity upon leaving the clinics. Participants registered close to a 5-point standard score gain on the Peabody Individual Achievement Test. In addition, upon completion of the program more than 50 percent of participants had either reenrolled in secondary school, enrolled in postsecondary education, obtained their GED, entered the military, or found employment. In the words of the evaluators: ". . . educational clinics have provided effective, low-cost services to teenagers who have dropped out of the public school system . . . and are worthy of public support" (*Report on Educational Clinics*, 1985, p. 42).

In 1987 Minnesota implemented the High School Graduation Incentives (HSGI) program. It provides students between the ages of 12 and 21 who have not succeeded in school with a number of "second chance" options. Students may attend public schools outside their district of residence or one of the 20 Area Learning Centers funded by the state or a private, nonsectarian, alternative school. In the first year of operation, 1988–89, approximately 1,500 students enrolled in the HSGI program, 700 of whom were school dropouts (Nathan, 1989b). In 1989–90 the number of students participating in the three HSGI options was more than 3,000 (Nathan & Jennings, 1990).

A 1990 survey of 943 students enrolled in the three HSGI options found significant increases in student satisfaction, school success, and educational expectations. The percentage of students expressing satisfaction with school increased from 25 to 70 percent, and 79 percent reported greater school success as a result of participation in the HSGI program. In addition, expectation of graduating from high school and pursuing some postsecondary education increased from 13 to 40 percent (Nathan & Jennings, 1990).

Conclusions about the relationship of "second chance" options to improved academic achievement cannot be drawn because results are limited to the Washington study. "Second chance" options do appear to promote diversity and equity, first, by increasing the educational opportunities for previously unsuccessful students, and second, by giving them a "second chance" at state or district expense.

POSTSECONDARY OPTIONS

Postsecondary options allow high school juniors and seniors to enroll in postsecondary institutions and receive both high school and college credit. In 1988 the state of Colorado passed the Postsecondary Options Act, which allows 11th- and 12th-grade public high school students to take courses at public institutions of higher education for high school and university credit. In its first year of operation, 1989–90, 407 students from 40 school districts took advantage of the new law. No evaluative data were collected from the students or participating institutions of higher education (Colorado Department of Education, 1991).

In 1985 the state of Minnesota passed legislation allowing 11th and 12th graders to attend public and private postsecondary institutions. Some 3,600 students participated in the Postsecondary Options Enrollment (PSEO) program during the 1985–86 school year. By 1989–90 participation had increased to 5,900 or about 5 percent of those eligible. A 1986 survey of students and parents indicated that 95 percent of students were satisfied or very satisfied with the

PSEO program, and 90 percent of parents felt their children had learned more than they would have taking only high school courses (Nathan, 1989b).

A more recent survey of Minnesota's PSEO program found increased satisfaction among participants. While 63 percent of students indicated satisfaction with their old school program, 90 percent expressed satisfaction with the new PSEO program. Thirty-two percent reported doing better academically as a result of participation in PSEO (Nathan & Jennings, 1990). The PSEO program has had an effect on some of Minnesota's school districts as well. More than 60 high schools have created new courses in cooperation with postsecondary institutions, and the number of advanced placement courses offered in high schools has quadrupled since the PSEO program began (Nathan & Jennings, 1990).

While surveys of participants in Minnesota's PSEO indicate high student and parent satisfaction and improved student academic performance, the self-report nature of the data makes conclusions about whether postsecondary options are associated with improved academic achievement problematic. Postsecondary options do appear to promote equity and diversity by increasing the educational opportunities available to students, but those opportunities are limited in states and school districts that provide no funding or only partial funding for students' tuition costs. Opportunities are also limited for students who do not live within commuting distance of a postsecondary institution or do not possess their own transportation. Finally, for the 50 percent of high school students who do not go on to any type of postsecondary education, including the 25 percent who drop out, postsecondary options do little to promote equity or diversity.

INTERDISTRICT CHOICE PLANS

Interdistrict plans allow students to choose from among most or all of the school districts within a state. To date, five states have enacted interdistrict plans: Arkansas, Iowa, Massachusetts, Minnesota, and Nebraska. Minnesota passed the initial legislation for its plan in 1985 and began implementation on a voluntary basis in 1987–88. Arkansas, Iowa, and Nebraska introduced interdistrict plans in 1990–91, Massachusetts followed in 1991–92. Four other states, namely, Idaho, Ohio, Utah, and Washington, have passed legislation to enact interdistrict plans beginning in 1992–93 and 1993–94.

Research studies on the effectiveness of interdistrict plans are few, and most of the data collected are descriptive rather than evaluative. In 1987 Minnesota began the nation's first interdistrict plan. School district participation in the plan was voluntary during the 1987–88 and 1988–89 school years. In 1989–90 school districts with more than 1,000 students were required to participate, and in 1990–91 all districts were required to participate. During the first year, 1987–88, 137 students transferred to other districts for their education. In 1988–89 the number was 435, and in 1989–90 approximately 3,200 students took advantage of the plan (Nathan, 1989b). At the beginning of the 1990–91 school year 6,200 applications had been received (Nathan & Jennings, 1990). Participation in the interdistrict plan has grown dramatically during the first 4 years, but it still represents less than 1 percent of the state's K-12 enrollment.

While the statewide percentage of student participation in the interdistrict plan is small, percentages among individual districts vary considerably. In 1989–90, 12 of the participating districts experienced enrollment shifts of more than 5 percent ("Most Minnesota Students Transfer for Convenience," 1990). Two of those districts, Mountain Iron-Buhl and Mound-Westonka, experienced significant declines in their student populations. Mountain Iron-Buhl lost almost 50 percent of its students when one of the district's two high schools was closed, and angry parents decided to send their children to a neighboring district rather than to the remaining high school (Pearson, 1989).

Critics of Minnesota's interdistrict plan fear additional districts will experience significant enrollment losses as the plan becomes mandatory for all districts. Their fears may be well founded if early results from Iowa's interdistrict plan are any indication. In 1990–91 only one third of 1 percent of public school students in Iowa transferred to another district, but 77 percent of those transfers came from districts with fewer than 1,000 students. In fact, 10 percent of the 1,674 transfer applications had to be denied because they would have exceeded the 5 percent enrollment loss allowed by law ("Across the Nation," 1990).

Minnesota, unlike Iowa, has no limit on enrollment loss. Its interdistrict plan could have a greater impact upon small rural school districts. The Minnesota House of Representatives research department conducted a survey of superintendents in 316 of the state's 433 school districts. Among superintendents in metropolitan areas, 9 percent felt their districts had benefited and 9 percent felt their districts had been hurt by the statewide interdistrict plan. Among superintendents in greater Minnesota, 23 percent felt their districts had benefited and 16 percent felt their districts had been hurt by the plan ("Minnesota Open-Enrollment Program," 1991). These results provide evidence of interdistrict plans' greater impact, positive and negative, on smaller, more rural school districts.

Depending upon the funding formula used, interdistrict plans can benefit some districts at the expense of others. In Massachusetts, districts that lose students to other districts must reimburse receiving districts at the rate they spend per pupil, even if that rate is higher than the leaving district's. In 1991–92 Brockton lost over $900,000 and Gloucester over $400,000 because many of their students transferred to more expensive districts (Diegmueller, 1991).

Although supporters of interdistrict plans assume that increased access to, and competition among, school districts will increase diversity and improve public education, the plans do nothing for students who are unable to leave their district. Virtually all interdistrict plans require families to provide transportation for their children to the boundary of the receiving district. Some states, like Washington, also require parents to pay all or part of any difference in property tax rates between leaving and receiving districts. Requirements such as these limit participation in interdistrict plans to those families which can bear these additional expenses.

Interdistrict supporters also assume that unpopular districts will "get the message" and turn things around academically, but it is not clear that these districts will be able to improve their educational lot if they lost significant numbers of their students and the revenue they generate. As Judith Pearson, a teacher in the Mountain Iron-Buhl School District observes: "Once a school district loses significant enrollment, an irreversible sequence of events is set into motion. The loss in revenue forces reductions in expenditures, which in turn will force reductions in programs and services. These reductions will probably prompt further enrollment losses, and so on" (Pearson, 1989, p. 822).

Even if a district can turn things around academically, there is no assurance families will remain. The fact is that most parents transfer their children for reasons that have little to do with academics. A 1990 survey conducted by the Minnesota State Department of Education revealed most families were motivated by convenience when making their decision to transfer to another district. Of the 1,234 families surveyed, 40 percent indicated their reason for transferring was either to be closer to home or to have a day care program. Twenty percent listed academic reasons for their transfer, and 6 percent said athletics and extracurricular activities were the reason for changing school districts ("Most Minnesota Students Transfer for Convenience," 1990). Similar results were reported in a 1990 Iowa survey ("Across the Nation," 1990).

Given the variety of reasons families have for transferring from one school district to another, it is difficult to assess the relationship of interdistrict plans to increased educational accountability. Additional research and evaluation are needed to establish whether interdistrict plans are associated with improved academic performance. While interdistrict plans promote educational diversity, concerns about equity remain. Their effect on smaller more rural districts is not yet known. In the meantime, states should proceed cautiously as they embark down the road of interdistrict choice.

CONCLUSIONS

As indicated at the beginning of the chapter, the disparity in quantity and quality of research on each of the choice options and plans is considerable. Drawing conclusions about the relative effectiveness of each is difficult, especially for "second chance" and postsecondary options and interdistrict plans. Only alternative and magnet schools and intradistrict plans have an adequate research base from which to draw conclusions with any degree of confidence. From the empirical evidence presented here, it appears that alternative and magnet schools combined with a "controlled" choice model hold the most promise for promoting genuine school improvement through increased educational accountability, equity, and diversity in public education.

Alternative and magnet schools promote accountability because of their relationship with improved academic performance and increased parent and student satisfaction. They promote diversity by providing a variety of specialized or thematic programs from which parents, students, and professional staff may choose. However, alternative and magnet schools promote inequity when access is limited by admission requirements, inadequate information dissemination, lack of transportation, or because there are not enough schools or programs to go around.

To avoid limited access a district needs to transform *all* of its schools into alternatives or magnets. It must base admission to these schools on student interest rather than on performance criteria or previous history of acceptable behavior. Every school should have a student population that is a cross section or microcosm of a district's total school population, including poor, minority, at-risk, and handicapped students.

The district must inform and educate parents about the specialized and thematic programs and provide free transportation to all of the schools. Lastly, alternative and magnet schools should be offered within the context of an intradistrict plan to ensure districtwide access. The "controlled" choice model is the most equitable because it gives all students and their families equal or at least proportional access to most or all schools within a district.

Although many districts have developed alternative or magnet schools and programs, few have attempted to combine them with intradistrict plans in any systematic way. In the next three chapters we will look closely at three school districts which have combined alternative or magnet schools and intradistrict plans in a comprehensive approach to school reform.

The three districts chosen for study are Richmond, California; Lowell, Massachusetts; and Montclair, New Jersey. The three range in size from small to large. All are urban and serve multiethnic student populations. The three districts have implemented intradistrict plans with varying degrees of choice and have experienced different levels of success achieving educational accountability, equity, and diversity.

Chapter 3 describes Richmond, California's "A System for Choice" experiment, which attempted to introduce specialty programs into all schools and make them available through an open enrollment model. Chapter 4 describes Lowell, Massachusetts' "controlled" choice model, in which zone and citywide magnet schools are available for student choice. Chapter 5 describes Montclair, New Jersey's "Freedom of Choice" plan, which combines districtwide "controlled" choice with the complete magnetization of all schools.

CHAPTER THREE

"A System for Choice"

Located in the San Francisco Bay area, Richmond Unified School District (RUSD) is the 16th largest school district in the state of California and enrolls some 31,000 students (1990–91) from the communities of El Cerrito, El Sobrante, Hercules, Kensington, Pinole, Richmond, and San Pablo. RUSD covers some 110 square miles and serves an ethnically, linguistically, and economically diverse population. Approximately 35 percent of the district's students are black, 31 percent are white, 18 percent are Asian, and 16 percent are Hispanic. More than 60 languages or dialects are represented. RUSD draws students from San Pablo with an average household income of $35,200 (1989) and from Hercules with an average household income of $60,200 (1989).

RUSD has historically suffered from poor student performance, low teacher morale, and financial instability. In a move born in part from desperation, RUSD's Board of Directors hired as superintendent the dynamic but controversial Dr. Walter Marks in the summer of 1987 and gave him a mandate to institute districtwide reform. Marks was chosen because of his experience developing magnet programs in Montclair, New Jersey and Raleigh-Durham, North Carolina. He had been forced to resign his position in Raleigh-Durham amid controversy regarding the district's misuse of federal funds; when RUSD's Board made its offer, Marks was superintendent of a small school district in Travis, Texas.

From July to December Marks conducted some 90 living-room dialogues with community interest groups to solicit opinions about the district's schools. One of the groups he chose to ignore, however, was teachers. The decision not to seek teacher input was made for several reasons. Marks had considerable experience designing and implementing magnet school programs and already had in mind much of what he wanted to accomplish in Richmond. He felt teachers were conservative and would resist radical change. Finally, given a limited time in which to act and the magnitude of the intradistrict choice plan, he believed that success depended upon swift and decisive implementation from the top down. In Marks's words: "This empowerment stuff is a bunch of crap. What we've done is, we've empowered people that are not practitioners in the business. The only people who don't have any power left are administrators" (quoted in Snider, 1989, p. 22).

Five pilot specialty programs were introduced in February, 1988. During the 1988–89 school year, programs were in place in 28 schools, and "A System for Choice" was born. In 1989–90, 19 more schools were included, leaving only 2 without programs during the 1990–91 school year.

"A System for Choice" has two main features, specialty programs and parental choice. There are eight specialty programs distributed among the district's 49 schools, namely, Applied Arts and Sciences (1 school), Classical Studies (8 schools), Futures Studies (8 schools), Gifted and Talented (19 schools), International Studies (8 schools), Montessori (2 schools), University Lab (4 schools), and Whole Language (1 school).

"A System for Choice" was designed, first, to improve the quality of education and, second, to promote ethnic and racial integration within the district. In the 1970s RUSD had attempted extensive forced busing to integrate schools, without much success. During that time districtwide enrollment of white students fell, teacher morale declined, and community dissatisfaction grew. For these reasons it was decided to implement a voluntary approach to integration that emphasized program quality and diversity rather than compulsion.

"A System for Choice" is a modified open-enrollment plan. Students are assigned to a neighborhood school but may attend any school in the district on a space-available basis. Students living in the attendance zone around a school are guaranteed admission to that school. Students wishing to transfer to specialty programs at schools outside their attendance zone register during a 2-week period in March. Applications are processed at the district office on a first-come, first-served basis. Siblings of students attending an out-of-zone school are given preference. A certain number of spots based on ethnicity are reserved at each school to promote integration. Students may not transfer to a school if the transfer upsets the school's racial or ethnic balance. Students and their parents are informed of their assignment by May 1. About 3,500 students apply for tranfers each year, approximately 75 percent of which are approved. Most of the rejections are because of lack of available space at the receiving school.

RUSD makes every effort to inform parents and students about the specialty programs and choices available. Every student is given a newsletter to take home, explaining the programs and application procedure. Information regarding programs and choices is published in the local newspaper. A bulk mailing of 90,000 information letters goes to patrons' homes. District-sponsored road shows are held at three of the five high schools. Each elementary school holds a meeting to explain the middle and junior high programs, and every middle and junior high school holds a meeting to explain the high school programs. In addition, special meetings are held in Spanish and Laotian for parents who do not speak English.

Transportation is very expensive for a district the size of Richmond Unified. Consequently, busing is provided only at the secondary level. Bus schedules for middle, junior, and senior high school students are made up by the district transportation office and are based upon school selection. Parents of elementary-age children must provide transportation at their own expense.

Specialty programs with more than one or two schools are distributed fairly evenly around the district. Students need not travel far to attend one of them. If a family is unhappy with the program or school in its area, it may attend another. All schools and programs within the district are open to parent and student selection. There are no admission requirements, and special-needs students participate in all of the programs. The eight models or programs are designed to be of high educational quality. A description of some of the more popular programs follows.

SPECIALTY PROGRAMS OF "A SYSTEM FOR CHOICE"

Classical Studies

The Classical Studies program (CSP) is located in six elementary, one junior, and one senior high school. Modeled after Mortimer Adler's Paideia program, the CSP is an option for intermediate and secondary students who want a prescribed curriculum; differentiated instruction featuring didactics, coaching, and seminars; a strong emphasis upon discipline; regular homework; and character development.

Two CSP schools are Sheldon Elementary and DeAnza High. Sheldon enrolls some 575 students, 56 percent of whom are white, 17 percent are Asian, 15 percent are black, and 12 percent are

Hispanic. Parents wishing to have their children attend Sheldon make an appointment with the principal during the previous spring, during which they sign a contract indicating understanding of, and support for, the requirements of CSP. One of those requirements is homework assignments of 30 minutes for primary students and 60 minutes for intermediate students, 4 days a week.

Students from kindergarten through 3rd grades are taught in self-contained classrooms by a single teacher and experience didactic instruction and coaching. Acquiring basic skills and essential information is the primary focus of the first 4 years of the CSP. Didactics, or teacher telling, and coaching are the main instructional strategies. Seminars are not introduced until the 4th grade.

All students receive 15 minutes daily exposure to character development. During this time students and teachers discuss weekly topics such as "aiming high," "the importance of respecting authority," "how to be a friend," and "respect for cultural diversity." All students are expected to follow a well-defined discipline code and to demonstrate appropriate standards of dress and appearance.

An integrated reading/language arts curriculum is introduced in the primary grades and employs IBM's "Writing to Read" program. Kindergarten and 1st-grade students are scheduled weekly into the computer laboratory with its 15 IBM-compatible computers. In addition to the required reading and language arts textbook, all students, including primary, are exposed to prescribed readings for the Paideia program. They include literature recommended by Mortimer Adler that is "important," "difficult," and "beautiful." Authors include Hans Christian Andersen, Ludwig Bemelmans, Emily Dickinson, the brothers Grimm, Langston Hughes, C. S. Lewis, Jack London, Scott O'Dell, Beatrix Potter, Isaac Singer, Mark Twain, Taro Yashima, and others.

The CSP becomes fully implemented in grades 4 to 6. Here the instructional methods of coaching and seminars are added to didactic instruction. At Sheldon, students receive a 40-minute period of didactic instruction in math followed by a 40-minute coaching period early in the morning each Monday through Wednesday. On Thursday and Friday social studies is substituted for math.

After morning recess, there is a 40-minute social studies seminar followed by didactic instruction in reading/language arts, Monday through Wednesday. On Thursday and Fridays, the seminar is in reading/language arts and the didactic instruction is in science. On Monday through Wednesday, lunch is followed by a 40-minute coaching session on reading/language arts and a 40-minute seminar on science. On Thursday and Friday, the coaching session is in science and the seminar is in math. The last two periods of the school day are completed by combinations of physical education, library, or fine arts. An after-school Spanish class is an option for 6th graders.

Coaching requires a student–teacher ratio of 10:1 or 11:1. This reduction of the student–teacher ratio is accomplished by assigning two instructional aides to a teacher's room during coaching sessions. A group of 10 or 11 students will sometimes go outside or to another classroom to facilitate studying. Coaching involves individual practice, tutoring, and small-group work. Students may work in pairs with the coach or teacher, or by themselves. Practicing what was taught and remediating skill deficiencies are the main focus of the coaching session. The classroom teacher typically works with students who are having difficulties or need additional attention, while the aides work with those who need less assistance or individual attention.

Seminars are designed to provide students with the opportunity to explore material in greater depth. Seminars take as their model the Socratic dialogue, which seeks to expose students to a "good conversationalist" who is skilled in asking intelligent, probing questions. Seminar classes average 16 to 17 students per teacher. This ratio is accomplished by dividing the class and sending half to a seminar teacher while the other half remains with the regular teacher. Sheldon and other CSP elementary schools have hired an additional teacher who does nothing but conduct seminars. Students have seminars with both their regular classroom teacher and the seminar teacher.

Work in seminars is not graded, and everyone is expected to participate. In math and science seminars, activities as well as discussions are used. Seminars give students and teachers the opportunity to explore topics in more freedom and depth. The smaller class size allows for less classroom structure and greater student–teacher interaction. Unfortunately, seminars and coaching require additional classroom space, which is not always easy to find.

At the high school level the CSP takes on added focus and increased expectations for students. DeAnza is the designated CSP high school for the district. It enrolls some 1,400 students, of whom 43 percent are white, 28 percent are black, 18 percent are Asian, and 11 percent are Hispanic. In 1989–90 DeAnza began the CSP for all incoming freshmen. In 1990–91 the program was expanded to include sophomores. The plan was to have the CSP fully implemented across all 4 years of high school by 1992–93.

The CSP at DeAnza features an expanded core curriculum. All students must take 4 years of English, foreign language, history/social studies, math, science, and Socratic seminar. Classes are heterogeneously grouped, which is to say, there is one track for all students. Students may move more slowly or quickly through that track, however. Some students may spend 2 years in algebra, while others move on to geometry the second year. To accommodate students who may have difficulty with the 4-year foreign language requirement, a skills course is offered prior to the traditional first year of foreign language, which emphasizes history and culture and a more gradual introduction to language structure. Electives and advanced placement classes allow students to pursue interests related to their gifts and talents. The CSP assumes that all individuals have an unlimited capacity for learning. What differs is the rate at which they learn.

The three instructional approaches of didactics, coaching, and seminars are incorporated in the CSP at DeAnza. Didactic instruction occurs in all classrooms and remains the most frequently used method of instruction. Coaching is accomplished through cooperative learning, small-group, and individualized instruction. Coaching is also facilitated through the use of computers.

DeAnza has a large four-room computer laboratory. One room is reserved for word processing, another for science, a third for math, and the last for miscellaneous assignments. Two full-time lab teachers assist classroom teachers in coaching exercises related to students' coursework. Students work on assignments, projects, and research. The student newspaper and literary magazine are produced there. The lab is well stocked with software for the 95 IBM computers, but the lab's two instructors are at a disadvantage in trying to assist 95-plus students. An additional instructor is needed to provide the optimum assistance to students and their classroom teachers.

Socratic seminars are held once a week. They are a time for conversation and exploration. Readings, works of art and music, and papers on science or philosophy, rather than textbooks, are the materials for seminars. Students are encouraged to offer their own interpretations of what is being discussed and not worry about whether the interpretation is the "correct" one or not. The teacher's role is less that of the expert and more that of the skilled participant who helps to guide the discussion and give it direction. All students are expected to participate and are evaluated on process rather than content. Students' seminar grade counts for 10 percent of both their English and history/social science grades.

Eight English and history/social studies teachers plus four extra teachers conduct the seminars. Extra teachers are needed to lower the student–teacher ratio. To facilitate seminars the school has scheduled English and social studies/history classes back to back. A two-period block with 60 students and two teachers is then available for weekly seminars. The extra teacher joins his two colleagues, and the class of 60 is divided into three separate seminars of 20 students each. Extra classrooms are needed at seminar time, which puts added pressure on a high school already operating at maximum capacity.

Even though it specializes in classical studies, DeAnza provides the full range of courses and activities of a conventional comprehensive high school. The district is committed to the comprehensive high school model and sees the various specialties as options within that model. The required core curriculum of 4 years of English, foreign language, history/social studies, math, science, and Socratic seminar does mean that students have fewer elective credits available to pursue courses in business, home economics, and industrial arts than do students at other district high schools. An optional classical-studies specialty diploma to have been offered in 1992–93 would have further restricted students' elective vocational credits by requiring individuals to complete additional credits beyond the district minimum of 225.

International Studies

The International Studies program (ISP) is designed to provide students with an understanding, appreciation, and acceptance of the variety of people, values, and cultures in their community and around the world. International studies is particularly important in RUSD, given its ethnic, racial, and linguistic diversity. The ISP is located in six elementary and two middle schools. Shannon is one of the six elementary schools. It enrolls approximately 350 students, 59 percent of whom are white, 18 percent are Hispanic, 13 percent are Asian, and 10 percent are black.

The ISP curriculum at Shannon is divided into three areas: core, elective, and concentration courses. Core courses include language arts, social studies, science, and math. Core classes are taught in the early morning and afternoon on Monday, Tuesday, Thursday, Friday, and all day on Wednesday. Primary students are taught core courses by their regular teacher in a self-contained classroom. Intermediate students are instructed in 100-minute blocks of math/science and language arts/social studies by two different teachers.

Elective courses in International Studies are offered Monday, Tuesday, Thursday, and Friday in four 40-minute periods from 10:10 AM to 12:50 PM. Students take one set of three elective courses on Monday and Tuesday, and another set of three different electives on Thursday and Friday for a total of six electives. A 40-minute lunch period completes the 160-minute time slot.

Students, with their parents' approval, sign up for the six elective courses three times a year. They indicate first through third preferences for each of the six electives and typically receive three first choices and three second or third choices. Course selection varies slightly from school to school. At Shannon students choose from approximately 100 courses offered each trimester. Among succeeding trimester courses, 75 are repeats and 25 are new. Students may not take the same elective twice, although they may continue the same course at an advanced level, such as in foreign language and instrumental music.

Concentration courses are extensions of electives and are for students who show a particular strength or demonstrate a high degree of motivation in a subject. Teachers and parents nominate students for concentration courses, and principals make the final decision. Electives in subjects like musical instruments and foreign languages become concentrations at advanced levels. A special concentration entitled "Create" is offered to gifted and talented students certified through the California State Gifted and Talented Education (GATE) program.

Elective and concentration course offerings are divided into three broad areas of international focus: technology, culture, and communications. Each of these areas comprises further subdivisions. Technology includes mathematical concepts and applications, computers, media, and science. Culture includes history, philosophy, political science, economics, geography, anthropology, sociology, and art. Communications is made up of language studies, composition, speech, and literature.

A catalogue of more than 250 elective and concentration courses complete with descriptions is provided by the district. In addition, district-designed unit plans and curricular materials for each course are also available. Course titles include "Arts and Crafts from Many Cultures," "Electric Eye," "Digging Dinosaurs," "Voyage of the Mimi," "Turtle Talk," "Media Magic," "Shutter Bug," "United Nations," "Dances from Many Lands," "International Cuisine," "My World and Welcome to It," "Let's Take a Trip," "Beginning and Advanced Instruments," "Hardhatting in a Geo World," "Track and Field," and "Calligraphy," among others. In addition, each ISP school offers from three to five foreign languages. French, Spanish, Japanese, Russian, and sign language are available at Shannon.

Courses are designed for 1st/2nd, 3rd/4th, and 5th/6th graders. Average enrollment is 18 in a class. Since districtwide class limits are 31 for primary and 33 for intermediate grades, 10 extra part-time teachers must be hired to teach the four-period, 4-day-a-week block of elective and concentration courses. Some classes enroll fewer than 18 students because of equipment limitations. Shannon has only 7 trumpets and 12 keyboards, so enrollment in these classes is fewer than 18. There are only five cooking stations in the home economics room. Each station can serve 3 students, so "International Cuisine" is limited to 15.

Finding extra part-time teachers for elective and concentration courses is not always easy. During the first week of the 1989–90 school year, substitutes had to teach some of the electives until qualified part-time teachers were hired. Fortunately, RUSD's location in the San Francisco Bay area gives it access to a large cosmopolitan population. Smaller or less well situated school districts might not be able to offer Richmond's extensive course selection.

Much of the instruction in electives and concentrations is provided by regular classroom teachers. Teachers are expected to develop a repertoire of four to six courses they can teach effectively. Although some rely heavily upon district curriculum guides, others are comfortable designing their own course offerings. Considerable talent exists among Shannon's teaching staff. One teacher has expertise in aerobics, two teachers are skilled in art, a fourth is a professional musician, another is bilingual, and one is knowledgeable about computers.

Finding adequate classroom space is a major problem when implementing ISP. Because the teacher–student ratio is reduced in elective and concentration classes, additional classroom space is needed between 10:10 AM and 12:50 PM four days of the week. Increasing enrollment at the school is causing a classroom crunch that may necessitate higher student–teacher ratios in future elective and concentration classes.

If the ISP has a drawback, it is extending the elective and concentration offerings to primary students. Although kindergartners do not participate in the ISP, 1st and 2nd graders do. It is not clear all

1st graders or their parents are ready to make choices and experience a variety of teachers. To accommodate the concerns of parents, the number of electives for 1st and 2nd graders was reduced in 1990–91 from six to four and the additional time given to the core curriculum.

Classroom limitations and participation by primary students not withstanding, ISP is a program with strong appeal for students and their parents. Students look forward to the classes they choose. The curricular variety is motivating for students who enjoy a change of pace. Parents of motivated or high-ability children are attracted to the concentration offerings which allow students to extend themselves and explore subjects in greater depth.

Gifted and Talented

The largest specialty program is the Gifted and Talented program (GTP) which is located in 13 elementary, 3 middle, and 3 high schools. The GTP assumes that all students have some gifts or talents worthy of encouragement and development. Participation in the GTP is based upon student and parent interest, not school selection.

One of the 13 elementary schools offering the GTP is Nystrom. It serves some 550 students, of whom 91 percent are black, 4 percent are Hispanic, 4 percent are Asian, and 1 percent are white. Nystrom is one of the older schools in the district and has a long tradition of strong neighborhood support.

The structure of the GTP is similar to that of the International Studies program (ISP). Students take their core courses (language arts, social studies, science, and math) in the early morning and afternoon on Monday, Tuesday, Thursday, Friday, and all day Wednesday. Students in grades K-2 have the same teacher for all core subjects. Students in grades 3–6 have separate teachers for reading and math.

Kindergarten students do not participate in the GTP. Students in grades 1 through 6, with parental permission, sign up for six Gifted and Talented courses to be taken between 10:10 AM and 12:50 PM four days a week. As with the ISP, students take three 40-minute classes on Monday and Tuesday and another three classes on Thursday and Friday. Some classes meet for two 40-minute periods because of the type of subject offered. "Woodwright Shop" and "Theatre Production" are examples of classes that meet for two periods a day. Students may choose from more than 100 courses including "Ballet," "Computer Workshop," "Kitchen Chemistry," "Be An Author," "Shopping Spree," "Magical Mathematics," "Gospel Choir," "Beginning Orchestra," "Culture and Art," "Rutabaga Baby," "Geography," "Let's Move," "Reptile and Animal Study," and "Popping With Power." Some ISP courses such as "Turtle Talk," "Spanish," "Shutterbug," and "Digging Dinosaurs" are also offered in both the GTP and the ISP.

As with the ISP, courses in the GTP are offered at both introductory and advanced levels. Aesthetics courses are introductory and correspond with electives in the ISP. Creative Individual courses are advanced and correspond with concentrations in the ISP. Aesthetics courses are open to everyone and provide an introduction and challenge for students in areas of special interest. Creative Individual, or "Creative I" courses as they are called, are for more able or motivated students and demand greater depth and commitment. Student enrollment in Creative I classes is by teacher and parent nomination and principal selection. Creative I classes at Nystrom include "Shutterbug," "Toyology," "Public Speaking and Debate," "Trumpet II," and "Advanced Spanish."

Aesthetics and Creative I classes are offered for a trimester. Nystrom students make their course selections three times a year. As with the ISP, students are grouped in multigrade classes for Aesthetics and Creative I courses. Most classes are designed for grades 1-2 or 3-4 or 5-6 combinations. Some classes, like "Team Sports," "Let's Move," "Orchestra," and other music offerings combine grades 4-6.

Like Sheldon, Nystrom hires part-time teachers for its broad range of Aesthetics and Creative I classes. Five part-time teachers including a computer expert, industrial arts instructor, professional choreographer and dancer, and scientist expand the GTP offerings beyond the skills and interests of the regular classroom teachers.

At the high school level the GTP takes on a more concentrated focus. Three high schools—two specializing in visual, performing arts, and humanities and one specializing in math, science, and technology—offer the GTP for grades 9-12. Pinole Valley High School (PVHS) houses one of the two visual, performing arts, and humanities GTP. PVHS enrolls some 2,100 students of whom 50 percent are white, 27 percent are Asian, 14 percent are black, and 9 percent are Hispanic. Like DeAnza, Pinole Valley is a comprehensive high school that offers the full range of academic, vocational, and extracurricular programs. In addition, PVHS offers an array of specialized courses and performance opportunities in the broad areas of dance, drama, music, humanities, and visual arts.

Students select survey courses in one or more of these broad areas. Those who wish to concentrate in an area may earn a specialty diploma by taking at least 60 credits within one of the five broad areas. A student wanting a specialty diploma in visual arts, for example, would accumulate 60 credits of coursework in painting, photography, graphics, drawing, or film. Many of these credits are in addition to the 225 credits required by the district for graduation, so individuals pursuing specialty diplomas must be highly motivated.

Students with a particular interest or talent may participate in one of the many performance groups. In drama there is a children's theatre group, an improvisational theatre group, as well as a large drama group which puts on six plays a year. In dance there are ballet, modern, jazz, and African-Haitian troupes. In music there is a marching band, symphony orchestra, a 95-voice and a 40-voice choir, chamber singers, as well as a barbershop quartet. These performance groups give numerous public presentations which have brought visibility and a well-deserved reputation to PVHS.

In the humanities students may choose from an impressive array of courses which include such titles as "The Personal Poet," "Mexican-American Literature," "French Experience," "A Living History of the Community," "The Creative Impulse," "Human Rights Now," "International Problems," "Dramatic Literature," "World Religions," "The Endangered Planet," "Law and Justice," "Black Literature," "Greek and Roman Literature," and "American Short Story."

The district has committed substantial monies to purchase equipment and improve facilities for the GTP at Pinole Valley High School. Improvements include a complete set of gymnastics equipment, a state-of-the-art keyboard room, complete lighting and sound equipment for performance areas, and remodeling of the visual arts rooms.

The GTP at both the secondary and elementary levels is open to any student who wishes to explore and develop a hidden interest or talent. Unlike most Gifted and Talented programs, the program in RUSD is inclusive rather than exclusive. Any student living in the attendance zone of a school with a GTP is guaranteed admittance. The program design is flexible enough to accommodate a variety of gifts and talents. Special-needs students participate in schools with a GTP, as they do in schools with other specialty programs. Different degrees of concentration and performance allow students to pursue work at levels that are comfortable and appropriate for them. Individuals have the option of surveying a few Gifted and Talented classes and courses or pursuing an interest or developing a talent in greater depth. The decision to do either is made by students and their parents, not by the school or district.

Futures Studies

The Futures Studies program (FSP) is designed to prepare students for the challenge of the 21st century by emphasizing problem solving and higher level thinking skills. Introduced midway through the 1989–90 school year, Futures Studies is RUSD's newest program.

Six elementary and two middle schools offer the FSP. One of the elementary schools is Ohlone, which serves 820 students of whom 46 percent are Asian, 31 percent are white, 13 percent are black, and 10 percent are Hispanic. The FSP attempts to organize the curriculum thematically. Subjects like spelling, reading, math, science, and social studies are integrated under a yearly theme such as "People," "Universe," or "Interdependence." Students and teachers in grades K-6 explore the theme from individual, group, and global perspectives in relationship to the present, past, and future.

Students are encouraged to learn through experimentation and research. To that end, students at Ohlone visit a Futures Center for several hours a week to work on projects related to the theme they are studying. The Futures Center is divided into three areas: an activity area, a computer lab, and a library research area. In the activity area a full-time teacher and the regular classroom teacher oversee a variety of hands-on activities which may include simulations, creative art, experiments, and performances. In the computer lab another full-time teacher works with the regular teacher to assist students to develop word-processing and data-base skills for experiments and projects. Thirty-three IBM-compatible computers are available for students to use. The library research area is staffed by a full-time instructional aide who helps students find books and materials for their research reports. Students visit the three areas for 1 hour each week.

A great deal of responsibility rests on the shoulders of the Futures Centers teachers. Their ability to work effectively with regular classroom teachers determines, in large part, the success of the FSP at each school. Futures Studies teachers provide inservice training to regular classroom teachers and assist in developing an integrated interdisciplinary curriculum.

Cultural awareness and foreign language appreciation classes are conducted by part-time teachers. Primary classrooms (K-3) are visited three times a week for 30 minutes each by one of the two cultural awareness teachers. Foods, music, clothing, and folk tales of various countries are typical topics of presentation. Intermediate classrooms (4–6) are visited three times a week by one of the two foreign language teachers. At Ohlone the language appreciation classes are in Spanish and Japanese. As with the ISP at Sheldon, finding qualified part-time teachers is not always easy. Turnover is high and some beginning-of-the-year scrambling frequently takes place.

Students are encouraged to develop problem-solving skills in the FSP. At the beginning of each day students undertake a 15-minute exercise called "What If?" Examples include "What if we had no thumbs?" "What if we had a third eye?" "What if we had to play the same game every day. What would it be?" and "What if people didn't need sleep?" The intention of this exercise is to get students to think divergently and to become more spontaneous in their contributions.

Problem solving is further developed through cooperative learning strategies. Students learn to work in cooperative groups, sharing information and practicing the social skills necessary to work effectively as a group. The final stage of problem solving occurs in the Futures Center as students work on a variety of group and individual projects.

The FSP has attracted considerable parent and student support in its first year and a half. During the academic year 1989–90 student transfers to schools with FSP increased by 5 percent, the most of any specialty program. It is not clear, however, to what extent the FSP was the main reason for the transfers. The program's newness, or its location in certain schools, may have contributed to its popularity. One factor that has influenced some parents is the perception that the FSP is a moderate alternative to the traditional approach of the Classical Studies program and the more radical approach of the Gifted and Talented and International Studies programs. Parents, especially those of primary-age students, seem to prefer the greater amount of time spent with the regular classroom teacher in the FSP to the pull-out elective classes of the GTP and ISP.

Adams Middle School

Adams Middle School is the flagship of "A System for Choice." It offers the International Studies, Gifted and Talented, and Futures Studies programs all under one roof. It is the only district school with three programs and is the only school with no neighborhood attendance zone. All students wishing to attend Adams must apply through the district office and are selected within the district's open-enrollment guidelines outlined earlier. Students at Adams represent the multiethnic and multiracial character of the district. Adams enrolls approximately 1,050 students of whom 39 percent are white, 36 percent are black, 15 percent are Asian, and 10 percent are Hispanic.

Adams, a former junior high closed for several years because of declining neighborhood enrollment, was reopened in 1988–89. The school was chosen for several reasons: The building was in reasonably good condition and could be refurbished cost-effectively. The school was located strategically between the hill and flatland sections of Richmond, making it geographically attractive to a variety of families. Lastly, Adams's reputation as an academically excellent junior high remained in the minds of district parents.

A new staff was selected during the summer of 1988. Although the principal could not personally choose her own staff because of seniority and transfer provisions in the labor contract, she did interview all teachers and describe the program to be implemented in the school. The principal also made all assignments within the school. Teachers chose to tranfer to Adams for a variety of reasons. Some wanted to be part of a new and exciting program. A number of teachers in the state-certified GATE gifted program transferred because of a district commitment to gifted education at Adams. Some elementary teachers came because they wanted to work with older students or teach a specific subject like art or music. A few teachers were attracted to Adams because of its academic reputation.

Parents selected Adams for a variety of reasons as well. Some were attracted by and committed to the program to be offered at the school. Others supported the strong parental-involvement emphasis of the program. A number of parents of gifted children followed the transfer of the GATE teachers to Adams. A few remembered fondly Adams's reputation as a strong academic junior high and hoped its reputation would continue as a middle school.

Once enrolled, students in grades 6 to 8 are assigned to one of eight houses of approximately 125 students each. Each house reflects the balance of race, ethnicity, sex, and academic ability, of the student body. Four teachers are assigned to each house and teach the four core subjects of English/language arts, science, math, and social studies. Teachers too are mixed, so both male and female and elementary and secondary teachers are found in each house. Teachers may or may not remain with a house and teach the core for all three years. Some teachers enjoy the challenge of teaching different grade levels of the same subject and follow their 6th graders through the 8th grade. Other teachers prefer to teach at one or two grade levels and remain with a house for a year or two.

The houses help to personalize a large school like Adams and make it less intimidating for students. A grouping of 125 is a reasonable number and allows students to get to know each other better. Assigning core teachers to each house facilitates cooperative and interdisciplinary instructional approaches. Teachers in one house had their students produce a "Book of Me" as an interdisciplinary project. In English/language arts students wrote autobiographies and personal-experience essays. In social studies students learned about immigration, past and present. In science students studied genetics and family characteristics. In math students analyzed population data and demographic trends.

The main attraction of Adams is the variety of elective Gifted and Talented, International Studies, and Futures Studies classes offered at the school. Students choose, with parental approval, elective classes from 12 program areas including cross-disciplinary, foreign languages, computers, language arts, math, media, physical education, science, social science; and applied, visual, and performing arts. Students sign up for six elective classes each semester, three of which meet on Monday/Tuesday and three on Thursday/Friday. Advanced classes in each program area are offered as well. Students taking advanced classes meet 5 days a week and may sign up for a total of three classes.

The offering of elective and advanced Gifted and Talented, International Studies, and Futures classes is extensive. A sampling of titles includes: "Logo," "Basic," "Word Processing" (computers); "French," "Spanish," "German," "Russian," "Japanese," "Chinese" (foreign languages); "Adolescent Years," "Drugs and Alcohol," "Odyssey of the Mind" (cross-disciplinary); "Great Books," "Literary Magazine," "Poetry—Publish and Cherish" (language arts); "Soccer," "Bicycling," "Gymnastics" (physical education); "I Hate Math Workshop," "Statistics and Probability," "Geometric Construction" (math); "Broadcasting for Radio," "Video Production" (media); "Environmental Ecology," "Genetics," "Botany" (science); "Black History," "Asian Studies," "Junior Historians at Work" (social science); "Dance Company," "Children's Theatre," "Keyboard" (performing arts); "Carpentry," "Electricity," "Cooking" (applied arts); "Crafts," "Cartooning," "Photography" (visual arts). Sixth graders must choose one PE class from their six electives, and 7th and 8th graders must choose two from their six electives to satisfy state requirements.

The array of elective and advanced offerings allows students to specialize and proceed through a variety of subjects at their own interest and ability levels. Some students may take 2 full years of a foreign language and begin high school foreign language classes at the sophomore level. Other students may complete Algebra II as 8th graders and qualify for Geometry as freshmen. Students with academic difficulties may take remedial electives in any subject to improve their skills.

Students also have access to two computer labs, one equipped with 30 Macintosh and the other with 30 Apple II GS computers. The emphasis on computer application from the elementary Futures Studies program is continued at the middle school level. A video lab is also available for all students but is used mostly by those in the media program electives.

Adams is committed to academic excellence in its curricular and instructional programs. That commitment has attracted an outstanding student body that is nearly 30 percent certified gifted through the state GATE program. Many parents, but especially parents of academically capable students, are eager to have their children enrolled in Adams. Evidence of that eagerness was a waiting list of 400 students to get into the school in 1990–91.

SUCCESSES AND FAILURES OF "A SYSTEM FOR CHOICE"

Although Adams is unquestionably an excellent school, its success has come at the expense of the other four middle/junior high schools. Adams's favored status as a school with three programs and no attendance area has given it an unfair advantage and resulted in high-achieving and motivated students leaving their neighborhood schools to enroll at Adams. When Adams reopened in 1988, highly capable students and their parents were actively recruited to ensure a successful beginning for the school. As a result, 8th-grade California Achievement Test (CAT) scores in reading, language, and math at two of the middle/junior high schools fell by more than 10 percentage points. CAT scores for 8th graders at Adams are considerably higher than those at any of the other four middle/junior high schools. The loss of these academic role models has made the task of administrators and teachers at the neighborhood schools more difficult.

In addition to inequities between Adams and the other middle and junior high schools, inequities still exist between the flatland and hill schools. Schools in the hill section of RUSD are viewed more positively than are those in the flatland area because the former serve primarily middle- and upper-income white students. This perception is shared by the flatland families who used "A System for Choice" to transfer their children to hill schools. In 1989–90 the five schools with the greatest transfer loss were flatland schools, while five of the seven schools with the greatest transfer gains were hill schools.

Inequities also exist among the eight specialty programs. As mentioned earlier, the Futures Studies program was the most popular program during the 1989–90 school year. The least popular program during that time was the University Lab program (ULP). Student transfers to schools with the FSP increased by 5 percent during 1989–90, while transfers to ULP schools declined by almost 6 percent.

The ULP was originally designed to take advantage of partnerships between local universities and the school. It failed to develop a clear focus and did not take advantage of the resources available at institutions of higher education. Consequently, twice as many students transferred out of ULP schools than transferred in.

Another program that has not achieved much popularity or success is the Applied Arts and Sciences program (AASP) at Richmond High School. The AASP was to begin in 1990–91, but its implementation was stalled by a lack of district funds. The AASP is designed to provide students with specialized practice in arts and sciences. The program features four production centers: Counseling and Personal Planning; Communications, Publications, and Media; Health and Fitness; and Technological and Environmental. Students receive job training experience in the centers that prepare them for the nonschool world. By mid-1990–91, however, only the Media portion of the Communications, Publications, and Media Center was operational. The failure to complete the other centers delayed full implementation of the AASP and hurt student recruitment. In 1989–90 Richmond High had more than twice as many students transfer out as in. Richmond High suffers from the additional disadvantage of having no feeder elementary or junior high schools for its program. Richmond High is the only school with the AASP and finds it difficult to compete with other high schools that continue specialty programs found at elementary and junior high schools.

Developing and implementing quality specialty programs is an expensive undertaking. In its move to put "A System for Choice" into place quickly and completely, RUSD spent all of its money and more. Near the end of the 1989–90 school year the district found itself in debt and had to borrow $9.5 million from the state to finish the year. A trustee was appointed by the state to oversee district finances for the 1990–91 school year. He soon discovered that RUSD's financial problems were considerably more severe than first suspected. The district's budget was out of balance by $23 million even before the start of the 1990–91 school year. The deficit grew to $29 million by midyear, forcing the district to apply for a second state loan. The magnitude of RUSD's financial problems and the need for a second loan resulted in the forced resignation of Walter Marks in December, 1990.

Governor Pete Wilson demanded suspension of the collective bargaining agreement between the district and its teachers as a condition for granting any loan from the state, a condition unaccept-able to teachers. Unable to reach a compromise settlement, RUSD declared bankruptcy in April, 1990 and ordered schools to be closed at the end of the month. Parents brought suit against the district in Contra County Superior Court and obtained an injunction against the early closing. The state was forced to loan RUSD $19 million so it could complete the 1990–91 school year as scheduled.

The causes of the financial difficulties were many. "A System for Choice" added an extra $9 million a year, or 6 percent, to the district's annual operating budget of $147 million. Teachers were granted generous salary increases of 9 percent in 1988–89 and 7 percent in 1989–90. In 2 years RUSD went from one of the top 20 districts in California to one of the top 10 in teacher pay. Teacher preparation time was increased from 100 to 160 minutes a week, and $500,000 for curriculum development was paid to teachers during the summer of 1989. Substantial amounts of expensive equipment were purchased for the various specialty programs. Additional adminis-trative staff were added at a cost of $1 million dollars a year. In addition, lower revenues from the state lottery, failure of an $8 million local parcel tax, and state withholding of $5 million in desegregation funds because of possible misappropriation reduced the district's projected income substantially.

While these expenses and income reductions caused most of the problems, other factors contributed to the financial shortfall. Rising costs and an inadequate system for state funding of public education in California had left RUSD without sufficient resources for a number of years. RUSD operated with budget deficits for 5 of the 6 years between 1985 and 1991. The district receives less money per student from the state than do similar districts. In 1989–90 RUSD received $2,930 per student, while nearby Berkeley and Dublin received $3,370 and $4,165 respectively (Schmidt, 1991).

The financial problems of RUSD are not unique but are shared, in part, by other districts. In 1988-89, 290 of California's 1,000 school districts spent more money than they took in. In 1989-90, 7 of the 10 largest school districts in the state had to cut their budgets (Freedberg, 1990). Public education, especially quality public education, is expensive. For large urban districts with substantial numbers of disadvantaged students, the financial burden is severe, particularly if the district is trying to implement fundamental systemwide change.

RUSD's financial problems resulted in the dismantling of "A System for Choice" during the 1991-92 school year. The specialty programs were eliminated, noncontract and part-time teachers who staffed the programs were let go, and the district's class size average was raised from 28 to 30. Administrative staff was also reduced to save money as RUSD began the painful process of paying off its debt.

Now that the 3-year experiment is over, what can be said about the success or failure of "A System for Choice"? Results from the state-administered California Academic Progress (CAP) tests indicate mixed success in improving academic performance. Between 1987-88 and 1990-91 the percentage of correct answers by 3rd graders in reading went from 75 to 73 percent and in math from 79 to 78 percent. Among 6th graders the percentage of correct answers in reading went from 68 to 74 percent and in math from 66 to 65 percent. The percentage of correct answers for 8th graders in reading went from 64 to 65 percent and were unchanged in math at 55 percent.

In addition to its goal of improved academic performance, "A System for Choice" was implemented to increase racial and ethnic desegregation. Results indicate that achievement of that goal was also elusive. In 1987-88, 28 schools had minority student populations that were either 15 percent above or below the district average. In 1989-90, 19 of those 28 schools improved their racial balance. However, 9 became worse.

RUSD's consolidation of seven very different communities makes desegregation especially difficult to achieve. It is one thing to convince parents to have their children leave the neighborhood for another school in the community. It is quite another to convince parents to have their children leave the neighborhood for a school in another community. RUSD's open-enrollment model, which guarantees admission to a neighborhood school, provides little incentive to desegregate. Space availability limitations districtwide also mean that only a small percentage of students are able to transfer to other schools.

The district's inability to bus elementary students hampers desegregation efforts further. Parents who wish to transfer their elementary-age children to other schools must provide their own transportation. This places a heavy burden upon parents, especially low-income and single parents. At the secondary level, where district transportation is provided, desegregation has improved. Most of the improvement, however, has been at the hill schools.

As mentioned earlier, hill schools are generally perceived more positively than are flatland schools. Although the district has been able to convince flatland families to send their children to hill schools, it has not been able to convince hill families to send their children to flatland schools. Some families sent their children to a hill school even when the school did not have a specialty program they wanted. For example, a student interested in science and math might attend El Cerrito High (a hill school with a GTP in performing arts) rather than Kennedy High (a flatland school with a GTP in science and math) because the former has a better overall reputation. Perceptions and attitudes formed over a long time are not changed quickly or easily. It will take a great deal of time before hill parents feel comfortable, if they ever do, in sending their children to flatland schools.

The one success of "A System for Choice" was the promotion of diversity through the introduction of quality specialty programs strategically placed throughout the district. The introduction and placement of the specialty programs increased access to quality public education, particularly for minority and economically disadvantaged students.

In the final analysis, however, the failures of "A System for Choice" outnumber its successes. The two main goals of improved academic performance and increased ethnic and racial desegregation were not achieved. RUSD's bankruptcy, however many its causes, must be considered a tragic failure on the part of the school board and the superintendent. Finally, the decision to develop "A System for Choice" swiftly, from the top down, without teacher input, was a major mistake that has left a reservoir of ill will among teachers, administrators, and school board members that is likely to last for years. Evidence of that ill will was demonstrated at the December, 1990 school board meeting, when hundreds of teachers in attendance cheered Walter Marks's resignation.

CHAPTER FOUR

"Controlled" Choice

Lowell, Massachusetts is located 35 miles northwest of Boston at the junction of the Merrimack and Concord rivers. Founded in 1821 by associates of the Boston Manufacturing Company, Lowell was one of America's first experiments in the industrial revolution. Abundant water power, cheap labor, and venture capital made Lowell America's first planned industrial city and the center of the country's textile industry from the mid- to late 1800s. Today, high-tech and service businesses are replacing mills as Lowell attempts to modernize and diversify its economy. Modernization and diversification are also coming to the city's public schools.

Lowell is an ethnically diverse, blue-collar city of approximately 105,000. Average household income is $43,300 (1988). During the last 15 years over 25,000 Southeast Asians, mostly Cambodian, have emigrated to the city, joining the ranks of earlier emigrants and their descendants, chiefly Irish, Greek, Portuguese, and Puerto Rican. Lowell's public school system reflects the city's ethnic variety. Of the 13,500 students enrolled (1990–91), 54 percent are white, 26 percent are Asian, 17 percent are Hispanic, and 3 percent are black. Fifty-two percent participate in the federal government's free or reduced lunch program, and 25 percent receive some form of public assistance.

In an early effort to meet the challenges of a rapidly growing and increasingly ethnically diverse school-age population, Lowell began a major restructuring of its educational system in 1979. Under the leadership of Dr. Patrick J. Mogan, then superintendent, and spurred by pressure from the Massachusetts State Department of Education to end minority isolation in its schools, Lowell developed a long-range desegregation and systemwide school improvement plan.

Lowell based its long-range planning on two previous and pioneering "controlled" choice plans. One was designed in 1971 for schools in Springfield, Massachusetts (by one of the authors of this book), a plan that was accepted only in part by the Springfield School Committee. The other was a plan developed in 1972 by the Minneapolis, Minnesota school district under the leadership of then super-intendent John B. Davis, Jr. The plan, the Southeast Alternatives Project, set up in one section of the city a system of alternative and magnet schools operating under a "controlled" choice student assignment policy.

When the original designers of the Springfield plan began working in Lowell in 1979, "controlled" choice became the basis for all long-range planning. In order to get started quickly and meet immediate state requirements for a desegregation plan, a magnet school approach was adopted as Stage 1 of the long-range plan.

A Citywide Parent Planning Advisory Council, made up of two parents from each school, was established. Teams of parents, teachers, and administrators were sent around the country to look at a variety of magnet schools in operation. When the teams returned, the Parent Council developed a systemwide survey to solicit from parents what kinds of magnet schools they would like to have in Lowell.

The two most popular choices were a microsociety school and a school for the fine and performing arts. In 1981 these two schools were established as citywide magnets. Five additional magnets were created that retained their neighborhood attendance areas but admitted students on a space-available basis. While the two citywide magnets attracted integrated student bodies, the five neighborhood magnets did not. Threatened with possible legal action by dissatisfied minority parents and pressured by the state department of education, Lowell moved in 1987 to Stage 2 of the long-range plan, an intradistrict "controlled" choice plan.

LOWELL'S "CONTROLLED" CHOICE MODEL

Lowell's intradistrict plan is a "controlled" choice model that eliminates the attendance boundaries of neighborhood schools and replaces them with two large attendance zones. The zones reflect geographically identifiable areas of the city, traditional school flow patterns, economical bus routes, and the ethnic and racial balance of the district. Zone 1 contains 10 schools and has a student population that is 51 percent majority and 49 percent minority. Zone 2 has 13 schools and is 55 percent majority and 45 percent minority. In addition to the 23 schools, the two citywide magnet schools and the high school enroll students from both zones. Applications for all schools except the high school have to be made at the Parent Information

Center (PIC), which admits students to individual schools based on a number of criteria. Enrollment at each school must reflect the ethnic and racial makeup of the school district.

"Controlled" choice is administered through the PIC on East Merrimack Street. The PIC is open Monday through Friday from 8:30 AM to 2:30 PM and on Thursday from 5:00 to 7:00 PM. A student assignment officer is in charge of the Center and is assisted by several bilingual parent-liaison coordinators who speak either Khmer, Portuguese, Laotian, or Spanish.

All parents must register their school-age children at the PIC. They fill out a student registration form and submit copies of their child's immunization certificates and evidence of date of birth. Parents must also fill out a certificate-of-address form and provide proof of Lowell residency. Parents of kindergartners register during a 4-week period in March. Parents of preschoolers register during a 1-week period in April. Both groups are notified of their children's placement by June 1. Parents of students new to the school district and parents of students wishing to transfer to another school begin registering on May 1 and are notified of their child's placement by July 31.

The school district conducts citywide school visitations for parents of incoming kindergarten students during a 1-week period in February. Individual tours may also be arranged anytime during the year. The school district makes an intensive effort to notify all families during January and February about the upcoming registration period. School officials make contact with hospitals, churches and temples, barber shops, ethnic restaurants and markets, shopping centers, doctor and dentist offices, and social agencies. Flyers are distributed in Khmer, Spanish, Laotian, Vietnamese, and Portuguese at a popular supermarket. Approximately 60 percent of the kindergarten and preschool children are registered during this drive. A second intensive advertising effort is made in May and June to reach the parents of the remaining 40 percent of kindergartners and preschoolers.

Parents indicate their top three to five school preferences on the student registration form. They may choose among schools within their attendance zone, as well as the two citywide magnet schools. Approximately 70 percent get their first choice, and 97 percent get one of their top three choices. Students are admitted to schools according to a number of criteria including space availability, majority and minority balance, sibling preference, and closeness to home.

The student assignment officer at the PIC takes parental requests and does a computer check to see if there is space available at the selected school. Space availability is a problem because children enrolled before "controlled" choice was implemented in 1987–88 were given the option of remaining in their current schools. This option plus strong enrollment growth in Lowell have created capacity enrollment in a number of intermediate grades at some schools. As these "grandfathered" children move through the system and the school district brings on line its eight new schools over the next 5 years, the space availability problem should ease considerably.

Assuming space is available at a selected school, the race or ethnicity of the applicant is considered next. Enrollment at every school must be within 10 percentage points plus or minus of the majority and minority percentages districtwide. If an applicant does not upset the ethnic or racial balance of a particular school, he is admitted. If space is available and ethnicity and race are balanced, preference is given next to applicants who have siblings attending the selected school and then to applicants who live closest to the selected school. Bilingual and special education students are assigned to schools at the discretion of the district, because every school does not have these programs.

Families that do not receive their first choice may appeal to the district's Appeal Board. The Appeal Board is made up of four parents, two each from the two attendance zones. Also serving on the board are the school district's desegregation project director, a parent liaison coordinator, a representative from the district's bilingual program, and three parents from the Citywide Parent Council. All decisions of the Appeal Board are final.

Parents may place their child's name on a waiting list for their first choice while the child is attending the second-choice school. Students on the waiting list have preference over subsequent new-student and transfer requests. Seventy percent of students on the waiting list are able to get their selected school by the second year. Interestingly, most of the 70 percent choose to remain in the assigned school after all.

Parents choose specific schools for a variety of reasons. Physical plant characteristics such as the newness of buildings, the spaciousness and condition of playgrounds, and the existence of hot lunch cafeterias are important to some parents. This is especially true in Lowell, where 18 of the 26 schools were built before World War II, and 10 of the 18 before 1900. Size or grade configuration is another consideration. A K–3 school with 250 students may appeal to one family, while a K–8 school with 650 students may appeal to another. The availability of all-day kindergarten or latchkey programs or the closeness of a school to a parent's workplace may also be deciding factors. Working or single parents may want a school with an all-day kindergarten or latchkey program to occupy their children from the early morning to the late afternoon. Parents may also want a school near their workplace to handle a child's sicknesses and emergencies more easily. Surprisingly, some parents choose a school because it is far from their home. This is because children who attend schools beyond a certain distance from their home qualify for free transportation.

Transportation to all schools is provided at no cost by the school district. A transportation specialist hired from a regional transit authority has computerized the school bus system to make it as cost-effective as possible. Intermediate students living 1½ miles or more from school and primary students living ¾ of a mile or more qualify for busing. In addition, students living near dangerous intersections (no sidewalks, heavy traffic) are bused regardless of distance. Afternoon buses also take children to private day care centers if they are located in the same attendance zone of the children's school. Massachusetts law requires school districts to provide busing for students attending parochial schools. Of the 18,000 students enrolled in public and private schools in Lowell, 7,000 are bused daily by the school district. Lowell contracts out its bus service to a national transportation firm at a cost of a little more than $1.9 million annually. The district, in turn, receives a little more than $0.7 million in reimbursement from the state of Massachusetts.

Parents are also attracted by educational programs at particular schools. A survey by the PIC found that 25 percent of parents chose schools for their educational program. Although Lowell does not yet have the variety or comprehensiveness of specialized programs that Richmond does, it does offer a number of options in the zone schools that are quite good, and in the case of the two citywide schools, outstanding. Among the better specialized programs in the zone schools are "The Write Connection" at Bartlett, Computer Assisted Instruction at Green, and Communication Arts at Abraham Lincoln.

SPECIALIZED PROGRAMS IN THE ZONE SCHOOLS

"The Write Connection"

Located in the Acre section of Lowell is Bartlett School. Historically the Acre has been the neighborhood of debarkation for newly arrived immigrants to Lowell. In the early 1800s the Irish were the Acre's first inhabitants. They were followed by Italians, Greeks, and, most recently, Cambodians. Bartlett serves new arrivals as well as long-term residents. The school enrolls 650 students in grades K–8, 46 percent of whom are white, 27 percent are Asian, 24 percent are Hispanic, and 3 percent are black. Seventy-five percent of the students participate in the federal government's free or reduced-cost lunch program.

Faced with a student body that needed improvement in writing and reading, teachers and administrators at Bartlett decided to concentrate on those skills. The theme "The Write Connection" reflects an attempt to improve writing skills through a variety of high-interest literature-based activities.

Reading and writing are encouraged through a number of special activities. In grades 4–6 a weekly story-telling session is conducted in classrooms, after which students are assigned related writing activities. The Community Reader program brings in community persons, such as city and school officials, legislators, and businesspeople who read to groups of children. The annual I Love to Read Week is a promotion featuring contests and prizes to encourage reading. In addition, the year-long Star Reader and Drop Everything and Read (DEAR) programs reward out-of-school reading.

Bartlett also has a Computer Pen Pals program that encourages writing through the use of computers. Every other week Bartlett students write to students in other Lowell schools using a computer and modem hookup. The Pen Pals program not only encourages writing but reinforces the word processing and desktop publishing skills students are taught in the computer lab.

Two facilitators, one in reading and one in writing, are assigned to the school. Their assignment is made possible by grant money. Bartlett has consistently been able to secure outside funding because of the energetic efforts of its administrators and teachers. In 1990–91 the school received over $200,000 in aid.

The facilitators assist teachers in developing writing and reading activities for their classes. The facilitators conduct demonstration lessons to introduce various writing and reading techniques to teachers and their students. They also serve as editors for the two newspapers published monthly by students in grades K–4 and 5–8 and assist with the publishing of a yearly anthology of students' written work.

Grant money is used to bring other consultants into the school. A children's author or illustrator visits Bartlett three times a year to promote writing and reading in selected classrooms. A second project, Child's Play, brings an author or illustrator to work with students in grades 1, 2, and 4. Each child writes a story with the help of the consultant and the regular teacher. One story is chosen from each of the three grades to be written and performed as a play in front of the whole school in the spring.

Bartlett has also implemented the Cooperative Integrated Reading and Composition (CIRC) program in the school. Developed by Johns Hopkins University, CIRC uses cooperative learning strategies to teach reading and composition skills. Bartlett brought in a CIRC consultant from the National Diffusion Network prior to the 1989–90 school year. The consultant conducted a summer workshop, a fall follow-up, and monthly visits during the school year.

Bartlett has also implemented some other programs not specifically related to writing and reading. A career program and business partnership help acquaint older students with the world of work. The career program provides 8th graders with career exploration through guest speakers and visits to businesses. Two local companies, Mercury Computers and Vaisaila, allow small groups of students to observe some of their employees at work so they can learn about what they do.

Bartlett has experienced considerable success with "The Write Connection." Results from the Massachusetts Basic Skills Testing program (MBSTP) indicate the percentage of 3rd graders passing the writing portion of the MBSTP increased from 80 percent in 1987 to 94 percent in 1989. The percentage of 3rd-grade students passing the reading portion of the test also increased from 73 to 85 percent. For 6th graders the percentage passing the writing and reading portions of the MBSTP went from 76 to 93 and from 63 to 84 percent during the same time.

Computer-Assisted Instruction

Located in the heart of downtown Lowell is Green School. Green was built in 1870, making it one of the district's oldest schools. It is also one of the district's smallest schools, with an enrollment of 230 students in grades K–3. Forty-three percent of Green's students are white, 31 percent are Asian, 22 percent are Hispanic, and 4 percent are black.

Green's specialized program features the use of computers to improve student learning. A computer lab with 25 Apple II E, five Apple II GS computers, and an extensive software library is located in the basement of the school. No specialist or teacher is assigned to the lab, although one 2nd-grade teacher is given monthly release time to order software, arrange the library, and write related lesson plans for software use.

All students use the lab regularly. Kindergartners go once a week, and 1st through 3rd graders go three times a week. Classroom teachers sign up their classes on the permanent schedule board outside the lab. Most of the lab time is spent reinforcing and extending information and skills taught in the regular classroom. Students work individually at a computer using software programs related to the classroom material. Much of the work is drill and practice, but students also produce projects and reports for class. Students are taught computer-related skills that vary in sophistication depending upon grade level. Kindergartners learn basic keyboarding, and 1st through 3rd graders learn simple word processing and graphics.

Occasional computer workshops are conducted for parents who want to see what their children are learning and acquaint themselves with the operation of the computer lab. During 1990–91 three after-school and two evening workshops were held. Parents were encouraged to bring their children to the workshop so the children could demonstrate what they had learned.

A major computer-related project was undertaken by teachers at Green a few years ago. They started a computer summer day camp for 100 children. Two sessions of 50 children each spent 2 weeks learning about and having fun with computers. The camp became so successful that the city decided to assist in its operation, expanding it and eventually taking the camp over completely.

Teachers at Green take advantage of the school's downtown location to introduce students to the city's history, government, and businesses. Frequent field trips to the police and fire stations, post office, city hall, *Lowell Sun* newspaper headquarters, and the historic mill complex are undertaken. Teachers are also able to take advantage of musical and theatrical performances at the Lowell Memorial Auditorium, which is close to the school.

A special feature of Green is its awards ceremony. After each of the three grading periods, the school holds an awards ceremony to honor successful students. Recognition is given for academic achievement, attendance, improvement, effort, and conduct. Approximately 75 percent of Green's students receive some kind of award. The ceremony is held during the afternoon at the Smith-Baker Auditorium adjacent to the school. Parents are invited and a substantial number turn out to see their children receive awards.

This school, which has been renamed the Murkland School, will move into a new building in September, 1992.

Communication Through the Arts

Abraham Lincoln School is located in the lower Highlands area of the city near a predominantly Cambodian neighborhood. The school enrolls 325 students in grades K–4, 47 percent of whom are white, 38 percent are Asian, 10 percent are Hispanic, and 5 percent are black. The specialized program at Lincoln is Communication Through the Arts, which emphasizes the teaching of oral and written communication skills by integrating arts into the core curriculum.

Communication Through the Arts assumes that exposing children to the arts not only promotes appreciation but develops critical thinking and communication skills as a result of that exposure. To that end, students at Lincoln are exposed to a wide variety of artistic experiences related to their work, particularly in language arts and literature.

Each grade level focuses on an arts theme throughout the school year. In kindergarten it is Rhymes and Poetry; in grade 1, Children's Literature; in grade 2, Storytelling: Folktales, Myths, Legends; in grade 3, Theatre Arts; and in grade 4, Visual Arts. Field trips, special performances and artists-in-residence expose students to a variety of arts related to the themes being studied.

The Boston Children's Museum is a source of field trips and curricular materials for kindergarten students and their teachers. Students learn multicultural rhymes and poetry. Poetry and rhymes are continued under the larger theme of children's literature in the 1st grade. Students experience the Enchanted Circle Theatre, which is a performance group that conducts poetry, storytelling, and related art workshops. The 2nd-grade theme, Storytelling: Folktales, Myths, Legends, is brought to life by performers from Indian Hill Arts, who present a program called "African Images." They conduct poetry readings and storytelling sessions, perform tribal rhythms, and demonstrate African mask making. A group of musicians called Flora DeCana performs songs from Central and South America. Each musician also discusses the language and culture of his native country in small group sessions. In the 3rd and 4th grades the themes of Theatre and Visual Arts are introduced. Each year the Groton Center for the Arts provides an artist-in-residence in either dance, puppetry, storytelling, or poetry. In 1990–91 the artist was a children's author who spent 6 weeks working with 3rd and 4th graders on story writing. Each child wrote three stories, one of which was selected for publication in book form. In addition to working with children, the artist conducted workshops for teachers to demonstrate writing process skills.

Daily instruction in reading is conducted by teachers in the afternoon rather than during the traditional morning period. Teachers decided to switch when they observed afternoon subjects like science and social studies were being shortchanged. They felt it was easier to make time for reading than for science or social studies. Switching reading to the afternoon forced them to make time. Additional activities related to developing communication skills include a 10-minute sustained silent reading period each morning. The school also participates in the annual Reading Jamboree in March, which awards prizes for reading books, and in the national Reading Is Fundamental program, which makes free books available to students four times a year.

Lincoln's efforts at Communication Through the Arts appears to be having a positive effect upon students' performance in reading and writing. From 1987–89 the percentage of 3rd graders passing the reading and writing portions of the MBSTP increased from 90 to 97 and 88 to 92 percent, respectively.

In 1991–92 students and staff at Abraham Lincoln, which has been renamed the Bailey School, will be moving into a new school building. Communication Through the Arts will be replaced by a new theme emphasizing International/Global studies. Planning has already begun, and teachers are developing the curriculum that will go into place when the new school opens in January 1992.

Other zone schools have developed specialized programs that are also quite good. Robinson Junior High has a two-way bilingual (Spanish) education program for 100 6th graders. McAvinnue School has infused cooperative teaching strategies into all of its K–8 grade classrooms, and Butler Middle School is developing a magnet program in technology to be implemented when the school moves to a new facility in 1992.

The degree of program development varies widely among the zone schools, even though every school has a school improvement planning team. Some schools have yet to conceptualize the program they want, while others have been implementing their program for some time. The administration has been encouraging zone schools to develop specialized programs that are distinct and unique from one another, but it wants teachers and principals to design the models, and decision-making by consensus takes time.

SPECIALIZED PROGRAMS IN THE CITYWIDE SCHOOLS

In 1981 two citywide magnet schools were opened to promote voluntary desegregation and provide alternative education programs. The two schools, Arts Magnet and City Magnet, are housed together in a specially renovated building that once served as a trade high school. The building is located in downtown Lowell adjacent to the historic mill complex operated by the National Park Service and has been specifically designed for the unique programs of the two schools.

Arts Magnet School

Arts Magnet is a K–8 school of 325 students, 63 percent of whom are white, 23 percent are Hispanic, 10 percent are black, and 4 percent are Asian. The percentage of white students is just within the 10 percent plus or minus majority–minority allowance for each school. Forty-five percent of Arts Magnet students participate in the federal government's free or reduced-cost lunch program, which is not much different from the district average of 53 percent. Arts Magnet offers an all-day kindergarten class for parents who need an extended school day for their child.

Arts Magnet is not an elite school designed to serve only talented individuals in the visual and performing arts. Students with artistic talent are not given preference over less talented students. All students, including special-needs students, may attend Arts Magnet. Admission to Arts Magnet is handled by the PIC, using the same criteria and procedures it does for all schools. Test results from the MBSTP reveal that 3rd- and 6th-grade Arts Magnet students are slightly below the district average for passing scores in reading, math, and writing.

Students at Arts Magnet spend a significant portion of the school day taking traditional academic subjects. K–6 students are with their teacher in self-contained classrooms, and 7th and 8th graders are with their subject-matter specialists. In addition to taking regular academic subjects, 7th and 8th graders rotate among industrial arts, PE, art, and music. Foreign language instruction is not offered at Arts Magnet.

Each afternoon from 2 to 3:15 PM all students go to an elective class to pursue their artistic interest. Students may choose from among five elective classes: art, photography/video, newspaper, music, and drama. To ensure informed choices, students must sample all five electives during the first 15 weeks of school (each elective class is taken for 3 weeks).

The activities undertaken in each elective class are varied. In art, students work on individual and group projects. Individual projects can involve weaving, ceramics, wood carving, or airbrushing. Group projects include designing advertising brochures for the local American Cancer Society, developing a logo for a Lowell Police Department special program, creating banners for the Lowell Children's Museum, and producing a piece of sculpture for the De Cordova Museum in Lincoln, Massachusetts. Older students are encouraged to enter a number of art competitions including the annual Massachusetts Art by Kids and the Boston *Globe*'s Scholastic Art Award. Arts Magnet students have been very successful in such competitions. For example, among the 50 winners statewide in the Art by Kids competition, 9 to 11 typically are from Arts Magnet.

In photography/video, students learn basic photographic techniques, how to develop film, and how to operate video equipment. A darkroom with film-developing equipment and supplies is available for student use. Students undertake individually selected and teacher-assigned photo projects. One assigned project was to take photos of new school building construction for administrators who wanted a visual record of the work. Another project involved a group of photo and art students that worked jointly with the art teacher to transfer photos to silk screens and produce a nine-color silk-screen print that was sold to raise money for the school.

A classroom wired for interactive television is available for the taping and transmission of lessons. One such lesson involved 7th and 8th graders from Arts Magnet and two other out-of-district junior high schools. Students from the three schools conducted a three-way TV conference on nuclear energy. Each school researched and presented a different topic. One school chose how nuclear power plants work. Another selected alternative forms of energy, and Arts Magnet dealt with the social aspects of nuclear energy.

Students taking the newspaper elective work out of the Apple computer lab where they learn desktop publishing and word processing techniques. Their major activity is the production and publication of a monthly newspaper for 7th- and 8th-grade students. Third graders also produce a newspaper, but do most of the work in their self-contained classroom.

In music, students sing in the choir or play in the orchestra. Two music teachers operate out of their choral and instrumental rooms. The instrumental room has electronic keyboards with sequencers and synthesizers to aid students who want to write musical compositions. The choir room is used for regular instruction and practice for the various school musicals put on each year.

Musicals are conceived and written primarily in the 8th-grade English class. The Rising Star Theatre (RST) was formed some years ago and produces musicals written by 8th graders and acted by 7th and 8th graders.

Musicals are rehearsed during the drama elective, as are occasional plays like *Love Incorporated*. Teachers from various disciplines work together to produce these musicals and plays. In addition to the contributions of the English and music teachers, the home economics teacher helps students make the costumes. The industrial arts teacher assists in building the sets, and the art teacher designs and paints them. A dance teacher also works with students.

During drama elective, 6th graders practice for their seasonal plays performed at Halloween, Thanksgiving, Christmas, and Easter. A drama teacher works with teachers in grades K–6 exclusively. Advanced students at all grade levels may be selected to act in a production by the Merrimack Repertory Theatre, a regional professional theatre company. In December 1990, 10 Arts Magnet students performed in *A Christmas Carol*.

In addition to the teaching staff, a variety of resource people provide enrichment in the arts. Professional artists, cartoonists, mimes, radio dramatists, storytellers, and musicians give workshops to students and assist in student productions. A pantomime, *Teddy and the Aliens*, and a radio drama, "Adventures of the Red Chicken," were two productions assisted by professional resource people.

Through the elective classes and visitations by resource persons, students receive frequent and varied exposure to art. The integration of art into the regular classroom, as illustrated in the production of musicals and plays, helps students see the connection between art and other disciplines. The goal of Arts Magnet is not to turn out professional artists but well-rounded individuals who have been exposed to, and taught, an appreciation for the arts. Arts Magnet appears to be successful in reaching its goal.

City Magnet School

City Magnet is the other tenant of the renovated trade high school building. Some 325 students in grades K–8 are enrolled in City Magnet. Fifty-eight percent are white, 29 percent are Hispanic, 7 percent are black, and 6 percent are Asian. Sixty percent participate in the federal government's free or reduced-cost lunch program. Like Arts Magnet, City Magnet offers an all-day kindergarten class.

Visitors are greeted by a sign on the front door which says Welcome to the City Magnet School, the Nation's First Micro-Society School. What awaits the visitor inside is a school unlike any other in America. The idea of a school as a microsociety originated with George Richmond, who experimented with the concept in his classrooms in and around New York City in the late 1960s and early 1970s. It was Richmond's belief that education "must be a dynamic process, one that will liberate students from a curriculum without any apparent fit to life, one that will orient students to jobs in the service industries and the professions, and one that will obtain for students a better appreciation of the world of experience" (Richmond, 1973, p. 189). Lowell expanded the concept beyond the classroom to include an entire school and created City Magnet, a miniature society based upon free market and democratic principles complete with its own economy, labor force, government, and laws.

The student body is divided into three clusters: primary (K–3), intermediate (4–6), and senior (7 and 8). Primary students are taught in self-contained classrooms by their grade-level teacher. Intermediate and senior students are each taught in cross-grade classrooms by a team of four teachers. From 8:45 AM to 1:50 PM daily, students acquire basic skills and information in their self-contained or cross-grade classrooms. This portion of the day is called the academy. The academy prepares students to participate meaningfully in the microsociety, which operates daily from 1:50 to 3:15 PM.

The microsociety and the academy classes are divided into four areas, or strands: publishing, economy, government, and science/high technology. The four strands correspond to the four academic areas of English, mathematics, social studies, and science/computers taught by the four teacher teams in the intermediate and senior clusters. In 7th and 8th grade, students also study home economics, PE, art, and music on a rotating basis twice a week.

In the publishing strand, students learn reading, language arts, and speaking skills that will serve them when they publish newspapers, produce plays, and make written and oral presentations. In economy, they learn the mathematics necessary to operate the banks and businesses. In government, students learn the organization and value of a democratic society so they can make laws and administer a legal system. In science/high technology, students study earth and life sciences and learn computer applications in data and word processing so they can gather and analyze data for projects and reports on environmental as well as other issues related to the publishing, economy, and government strands of the microsociety.

Many of the lessons taught in the academy are drawn from activities in the microsociety. Putting together a news article, computing profit and loss for a business, getting a new law passed or a student punished, and collecting and analyzing salary data, taxes, and court fines take on real meaning when students face these problems and tasks daily in the microsociety.

All students in grades 4 through 8 hold jobs within the microsociety system. Students must pass placement exams to qualify for an occupation. The more responsible the occupation the higher the exam score required. Students are expected to hold at least one job in each of the four strands before graduation. From kindergarten through third grade, students do not have assigned jobs. Third graders observe older students so they will be better prepared to work when they become 4th graders. Kindergartners through 2nd graders spend most of their time in the primary cluster of microsociety, undertaking teacher-initiated projects and learning to be good citizens. Their forays into the larger microsociety are more teacher controlled.

Jobs in microsociety are many and varied. In publishing they include yearbook, senior newspaper, primary publishing, theatre production, and gossip magazine; in economy they include stationery store, art gallery, banking, holding company, primary store, and crafts or woodwork manufacturing; in government, jobs include legislative staff, lawyers, crime stoppers, community services, treasury and lottery departments, primary and intermediate/senior courts; and in science/high-technology they include computer marketplace, computer resource center, and data processing.

Microsociety operates by the student-written rules of a "City Magnet Constitution and Laws." The student written constitution provides for a democratic form of government with executive, legislative, and judicial branches. A president and VP are chosen schoolwide by kindergarten through 8th-grade students and together with City Magnet's principal constitute the executive branch. A 28-member student legislature (4 from the primary and 12 each from the intermediate and senior clusters) constitute the legislative branch. Second through 8th graders vote for representatives. A primary court and an intermediate/senior court comprise the judicial branch. Judges and lawyers, all of whom have passed the schools bar exam, are appointed by teachers and come from grades 4–8.

Governmental responsibilities include providing a minimum income for citizens, levying taxes and granting licenses, trying civil and criminal cases, passing new laws, and policing crime. Each citizen is paid between 100–200 Mogans a week depending upon the job held (the Mogan is the currency unit used in microsociety and is named after Dr. Patrick J. Mogan, superintendent of Lowell Public Schools when City Magnet School opened in 1981).

All citizens pay 40 Mogans a week tuition for their academy classes, and an income tax of 15 Mogans a week to support government services. Licenses to operate businesses cost 50 Mogans; patents cost 35 Mogans. Microsociety laws are enforced by crime stoppers who monitor the activity session for loitering, littering, eating, and inappropriate behavior. Violators are fined 50 Mogans for each offense.

The legislature confronts a number of issues annually. Taxation is a perennial one. Some representatives consider the flat tax of 15 Mogans unfair and want to replace it with a progressive income tax. Which services to provide and at what cost is another issue. During the 1988–89 school year the PTO donated $500 for library books. When it became time to hire a student to help the librarian, a publishing teacher reminded students that libraries were a government responsibility. Student representatives responded, and the legislature set up a budget and hired student librarians.

A major issue occurred during the 1989–90 school year, when the vice president proposed a soda pop machine to be located near the cafeteria. Discussion in the legislature drew upon research from the science/high technology strand regarding the nutritional value of soda beverages. An amended proposal was passed to request a fruit juice machine instead. After the machine was installed, citizens were hired to order juices, keep records, and pay bills. After a few weeks, however, a judicial review committee discovered that the juice machine was in possible violation of the federal government's lunch program. Letters to the local congressman from microsociety's president and other students led to further clarification and a decision from Washington, DC, that fruit juice was nutritional and could be sold during lunch periods in the school cafeteria.

Court cases covering a wide variety of infractions are heard weekly. The supreme court hears rare constitutional arguments and meets only occasionally. The primary and intermediate/senior courts hear civil and criminal cases brought by the government and private citizens. It costs 250 Mogans to file a suit.

Some illustrative cases include the bullying of a primary student by an intermediate student on the school bus. An older student helped the primary student fill out the complaint and obtain a lawyer. During the trial the defendant confessed and was sentenced to a week of lost recess time. Another case involved a 6th-grade girl who was being harassed in school by a 6th-grade boy. Her lawyer took the defendant to criminal court and obtained a conviction. The defendant was penalized 600 Mogans. The girl's lawyer then filed suit in civil court and won a judgment of 750 Mogans. A third case was a disputed lease agreement between a holding company and small business in the marketplace. A holding company had contracted out its space to a company that wanted to sell decorations in the marketplace. A second company took down the decorations before the first company's lease expired. The holding company sued the second company and was awarded damages. A controversial case during the 1989–90 school year involved the principal and the senior newspaper. The newspaper printed an uncomplimentary photo the principal judged to be in poor taste. The principal made her opinion known publicly, and the newspaper staff responded with a suit alleging unfair criticism. The newspaper lost its case.

The economic heart of microsociety is the marketplace. Numerous businesses operate in a large open area in the basement of the school. Small businesses sell decorations, toys, buttons, signs; stationery items like paper, pencils, and erasers; flowers; and other objects. Two banks, several legal firms, and some larger businesses share space alongside the small businesses in the marketplace. Some of the businesses are ongoing from year to year (the stationery store). Others are the result of individual entrepreneurship (Dave's Flower Shop). Some are conceived in the classroom with teacher encouragement and assistance (wooden locker shelves produced by an industrial arts class).

The banks, Magnet Institute for Savings and City Magnet Central Bank, are the financial centers of microsociety. They compete for depositors and make loans to businesses. Every citizen has a passbook savings account, and wages are deposited weekly to their account. City Magnet Bank serves as the reserve bank for the microsociety and controls the money supply.

Data processing tasks related to the marketplace, such as payroll, billings, loan payments, and bank interest are done on computers by students who have passed the qualification exams. A lab of 24 Apple II GS and another of 7 Macintosh computers provide the necessary hardware and software. The bimonthly senior newspaper, *Gazette*, is published out of the Macintosh lab and sells for 30 Mogans.

Like all societies, microsociety is not perfect. Some citizens, especially the youngest ones, do not always have a clear and complete grasp of what they are supposed to be doing. Some employees do not take their jobs as seriously as others. Off-task behavior can be observed in the marketplace. When asked about these imperfections, teachers reply "City Magnet is not a finished product but a work in progress." To encourage on-task behavior, students receive a grade in microsociety based upon a checklist of behaviors. In addition, upon admission students must have their parents read and sign a home-school partnership agreement that defines the responsibilities of students, parents, and teachers. High expectations are placed upon parents as well as students and teachers.

The application of knowledge and skills from the academy to the microsociety allows students to see the connection between school and life. Learning becomes immediate and real, resulting in levels of enthusiasm, energy, and participation among students rarely found in other schools.

The success of microsociety has brought City Magnet national attention and critical acclaim. The school has been featured on national television and has been the subject of numerous newspaper and journal articles. While such publicity is appreciated by the administrators and teachers at City Magnet, the most important endorsement they receive is the one from parents and students in Lowell. The annual waiting list of more than 150 is City Magnet's ultimate compliment and measure of success.

It is clear from the descriptions of Arts and City Magnet that the specialized programs at the citywide schools are at present more comprehensive than those at the zone schools. Part of the reason for the difference is the length of time schools have had to develop their programs. Arts and City Magnet have been refining their programs since 1981, while some of the zone schools are in the initial stages of program development. In addition, the two citywide schools have resources available to them that are not available in the same degree to the zone schools. Arts and City Magnet each have an on-site facilitator to assist the school with program development and to teach part-time. The 23 zone schools, on the other hand, must share five district facilitators among them. Arts and City Magnet also receive approximately $16,000 each from the district for program development, compared with $5,000 each for the zone schools.

Arts and City Magnet are the district's flagships and will remain so, but the administration is attempting to distribute resources more equitably to the zone schools. Between 1992 and 1996, Lowell will build eight new schools. Each school will feature a specialized program that is distinct and unique. Among the programs being planned are Humanities, International, Math/Science, Communications, and Futures and Technology. Teachers and administrators, along with district facilitators, have begun planning the programs for the new schools to be opened in 1992–93. Money has been made available for teacher release time and the hiring of consultants. The intent is to develop programs that will compete effectively with Arts and City magnet. In addition, the district has undertaken a pilot project with the University of Lowell to add a third citywide school.

The University of Lowell Demonstration School

The pilot project is the University of Lowell Demonstration School for children aged 3–5. Begun in the fall of 1990, the school is a joint venture of Lowell Public Schools and the College of Education at The University of Lowell. Three teachers and a director operate out of two large rooms and a small office in Read Hall on the university's west campus in North Chelmsford.

The Demonstration School is designed to serve a multilingual, culturally and economically diverse student body and to model effective approaches to teaching and teacher education for urban education. Forty students aged 3–5, 70 percent of whom participate in the federal government's free or reduced-cost lunch program, were selected from a list of interested parents by the PIC. Twenty of the students speak English, 10 speak Spanish, and 10 Khmer. The three teachers are also culturally and linguistically diverse. One is Cambodian, a second is Puerto Rican, and a third is Anglo. The director is Chinese American.

A central belief of the Demonstration School is that language awareness and acquisition are best accomplished at an early age. A major goal is to have all students master written and oral English. A second goal is to reinforce non-English-speaking students in their native language while they are learning English. A third goal is to expose English-speaking students to foreign languages. The Demonstration School does not advocate a particular educational philosophy, but it does embrace many of the characteristics of open education such as choice periods, learning centers, developmentally appropriate materials, an emphasis upon outside play and exploration, studio art and music, and whole language instruction.

The school day begins with play from 9 to 10 AM followed by clean up, music, and calendar. Language arts follows from 10 to 11 AM and includes reading and story writing. Khmer- and Spanish-speaking students are in their own groups at this time. Choice, music, and recess are staggered between 11 and 11:30 AM. At 12 PM, 3-year-olds and immature 4-year-olds go home. Five-year-olds and mature 4-year-olds have lunch and take a nap untl 1 PM. From 1 to 1:30 PM students have Spanish and Khmer instruction, switching from one to the other after 15 minutes. Math is from 1:30 to 2 PM, followed by choice from 2 to 3 PM and the end of the day.

Eventually the Demonstration School will be equipped with computers, video tapes, laser discs, and interactive television capabilities for both student and teacher use. The Demonstration School will enable student teachers from the University of Lowell, as well as teachers and administrators from Lowell, to observe and practice effective teaching strategies. Faculty members at the University of Lowell will be able to conduct research using the demonstration school as a laboratory. New, larger quarters were built on the campus in 1992. Over the next 4 years enrollment will increase to 200 K–4 students and the staff to 16 teachers.

The Demonstration School provides the Lowell School District with a number of educational benefits. First, it affords the district an excellent opportunity to expand and improve its early-childhood and bilingual education programs. Currently, the district has no bilingual preschool program and, given the continuing influx of immigrants, feels a need to develop such a program. Second, it is a source of well-trained early-childhood teachers. The eight new schools to be brought on line by 1996 will be either pre-K–4 or 5–8 schools. Lowell anticipates a need for new teachers, especially in the pre-K–4 schools. Third and last, the creation of the Demonstration School helps to ease the district's space availability problems.

STRENGTHS AND WEAKNESSES OF LOWELL'S "CONTROLLED" CHOICE MODEL

The main strength of Lowell's "controlled" choice plan has been its ability to promote both equity and system-wide educational diversity and school improvement. The implementation of "controlled" choice has also resulted in improved racial and ethnic desegregation. Prior to implementation, 11 of the district's 26 schools were out of compliance with state and federal desegregation guidelines. Four of the 11 were significantly imbalanced. Two had enrollments that were more than 90 percent majority, and two had enrollments that were more than 70 percent minority. By 1990–91 only four schools remained imbalanced, and all four were within 5 percentage points of the district's guidelines. The centralized admission process of the PIC and the provision of free transportation for all students have been the key factors in successful desegregation.

Balancing racial and ethnic percentages at each school is not easy given the demographic changes in Lowell's school-age population. When "controlled" choice was implemented in 1987, the district was 68 percent majority and 32 percent minority. In 4 years that ratio has changed to 54 percent majority and 46 percent minority. In order to balance the schools, the PIC has begun to place some students in schools out of their zone. This practice is expected to increase, and as it does, the line between zone 1 and zone 2 schools will become blurred. Eventually, the distinction between the two zones will have to be eliminated, and all schools will become citywide rather than zone schools.

Lowell's "controlled" choice model is also associated with improved academic performance. Since the implementation of "controlled" choice in 1987, the percentage of students passing the reading, writing, and math portions of MBSTP has increased. Test results for 3rd, 6th, and 9th graders (the three grade levels tested) indicate 88 percent of 3rd graders passed the reading portion, 83 percent passed writing, and 89 percent passed math in 1987. In 1989 the percentages were 91 percent (reading), 90 percent (writing), and 93 percent (math). In 1987, 72 percent of 6th graders passed the reading portion, 78 percent passed writing, and 83 percent passed math. In 1989 the percentages were 83 percent (reading), 91 percent (writing), and 91 percent (math). In 1987, 72 percent of 9th graders passed the reading portion, 79 percent passed writing, and 79 percent passed math. In 1989 the percentages were 79 percent (reading), 84 percent (writing), and 80 percent (math).

In addition to the association with improved academic performance and increased ethnic and racial desegregation, "controlled" choice has institutionalized parent participation in the educational process. Parents make their views known at the district level through the Citywide Parent Council, which is made up of two voting members from each of the district's schools. The council's primary role is to be an advocate for public education in Lowell. It makes recommendations to the school committee in a variety of areas including school buildings, educational standards, minority isolation, and school curricula. Council members sit on the PIC, the Appeal Board, the school district's building committee, and the district's interviewing committee for new teachers and administrators. The council is active politically and endorses candidates for the school committee.

Finally, "controlled" choice has increased the involvement of teachers and principals in program development and implementation. Each school has a steering committee made up of the principal and interested teachers. The main responsibility of the steering committee is to decide how to spend state and federal desegregation monies that have been allocated. Five districtwide facilitators provide assistance to the steering committees of the 23 zone schools, and two on-site facilitators assist Arts and City Magnet Schools. The facilitators provide inservice and help in locating consultants and resources to improve a school's particular programs.

Each school is responsible for designing and implementing its own theme. The district provides release time to allow teachers and principals to meet during the school day for program planning. At the eight schools scheduled for new buildings, long-range planning committees of parents, teachers, and principals have been established and already are at work developing the specialized programs that will be featured in their schools.

Lowell's decentralized approach to program development is the brain child of superintendent George Tsapatsaris, who wants parent, teacher, and principal participation in curricular and instructional reform. Although recently appointed in January 1991, Tsapatsaris served for many years as a teacher and principal in Lowell and knows the district's schools and staff very well. Prior to his appointment, he was project director of the district's "controlled" choice desegregation plan. It was under his directorship that steering committees in each school were established.

Tsapatsaris' cooperative approach is a reflection not only of his management philosophy, but also of the political realities of the Lowell School District. Teachers have a strong union organization, and principals are appointed to a specific school by the school committee rather than by the superintendent, although all such appointments must be recommended by the superintendent. Superintendents may determine new hires and transfer requests, but they may not remove or transfer principals against their will. To be successful in instituting reforms, a superintendent must possess considerable powers of persuasion.

One weakness of Lowell's "controlled" choice model at the present time is the promotion of educational diversity. The decision to make program development the responsibility of each school has resulted in unevenness in the comprehensiveness and quality of themes and specialized programs from school to school. From the program descriptions presented earlier in the chapter, it is clear that Arts and City Magnet have more comprehensive and higher quality programs than do zone schools. Increased attention is now being given to developing high-quality specialized programs in all zone schools. Some of the unevenness will also disappear as the eight new schools are brought on line and the Demonstration School expands its enrollment, but further work still needs to be done to upgrade and develop more fully diverse programs in the remaining 19 zone schools.

Curricular and instructional changes will not come instantly, however. The decision to involve parents, teachers, and principals in program development means that Lowell will not rush into implementing change as quickly and decisively as Richmond, California did with its top-down approach. Shared decision making takes time. Some of Lowell's teachers and principals have not had experience developing programs and need additional time as they learn on the job.

Although perhaps less exciting to those who would like to see educational change implemented quickly and decisively, Lowell's cautious, deliberate, and collaborative approach may prove wiser in the long run. The district is laying a solid foundation on which to build systemwide school improvement, a foundation that should remain long after individual superintendents come and go. The decision to institutionalize important roles for principals, teachers, and parents gives the various participants a vested interest in seeing that choice succeeds now and in the future.

CHAPTER FIVE

"Freedom of Choice"

Montclair, New Jersey is a bedroom community of 38,000 located 12 miles from New York City. The city's population is approximately 70 percent white and 30 percent minority and consists of Wall Street managers, New York media and insurance executives, as well as blue-collar and service industry workers. Average household income is $108,400 (1990).

Montclair's public schools enroll approximately 5,550 students (1990–91), 48 percent of whom are white, 46 percent are black, 4 percent are Asian, and 2 percent are Hispanic. Numerous private and parochial schools in the surrounding area attract white students, leaving the public schools with a higher percentage of minority students than is found in the community at large.

Achieving and maintaining racial balance has been a major commitment of Montclair for the last 20 years. In the early 1970s the district found itself faced with a state court order to desegregate its school system. Montclair's first response was to introduce forced busing from 1972 to 1976. During those 4 years tensions ran high, and more white families enrolled their children in private and parochial schools. In 1977 the district discontinued forced busing and introduced magnet schools under the leadership of Walter Marks, who was later to develop Richmond, California's "A System for Choice." A Gifted and Talented program was placed in an elementary school with predominantly black enrollment to draw white students, and a Fundamental magnet was established in an elementary school with a predominantly white enrollment to attract black students.

The magnet approach worked successfully for about 5 years. By the early 1980s, however, increasing minority enrollments and a decline in majority enrollments caused the districtwide percentage of minority students to increase to nearly 50 percent. In addition, parents expressed concern about the fairness of spending more money on magnet schools than on neighborhood schools. In 1985 the school district introduced "Freedom of Choice," which transformed all schools into districtwide magnets to be selected by parents and students through a "controlled" choice model.

Beginning with the 1985–86 school year, Monclair eliminated the neighborhood attendance boundaries of its elementary and middle schools (the district has only one high school). Parents now must register their children at the district's central office on Valley Road and indicate their top two school preferences. In addition to filling out the registration form, parents must provide a copy of the child's birth certificate, proof of residency, and evidence of immunizations. Applications for 4-year-olds (Montclair offers prekindergarten classes in all of its schools) and new students K–8 are available on March 1. Registration is during the second week of March, although students may enroll throughout the year. Families are notified of prekindergarten placements on May 1. Ninety-five percent of applicants get either their first or second choice. "Freedom of Choice" applications for students currently in grades pre-K–8 and new K–8 wishing to transfer are available on April 1. Families are notified about transfer placements on July 1. Approximately 100 students transfer each year; most of the transfers occur between grades 5 and 6.

Three criteria for school placements are applied by the district secretary, who processes all parental requests. First is space availability at the school selected, second is ethnicity or race of the applicant, and third is whether the applicant has siblings at the selected school. Assuming that space is available at a particular school, an applicant is admitted if the placement does not upset the school's racial or ethnic balance. All schools must be within 10 percentage points plus or minus of the districtwide averages for minority and majority student enrollment. If space is available and ethnicity and race are balanced, preference is given to applicants who have siblings attending the selected school. Families that do not receive their first choice may appeal to the assistant superintendent, who makes all final decisions. The district keeps a waiting list for individual schools through September 30.

The school district conducts an extensive advertising campaign to inform all families about the "Freedom of Choice" plan and the specialized programs at the various schools. In January the superintendent meets with private nursery school and Headstart directors. The directors provide the district with a list of kindergarten parents to be called and informed about the March registration dates. In February the superintendent meets with the Montclair Board of Realtors to explain "Freedom of Choice" and answer any questions.

During this month the district publicizes the plan and registration dates through advertisements in the local newspaper, articles in the district's monthly newsletter, and information handouts students take home to their parents. In addition, an elementary orientation meeting is held at one of the centrally located schools to describe the various magnet programs and answer parents' questions. In March, the week prior to registration for all new students, all schools are open for visitations by parents and interested patrons. Registration for prekindergarten is conducted during the second week of March from 1:00 to 9:00 PM.

Families in Montclair choose particular schools for a variety of reasons. Transportation is one of them. Like Lowell, the district contracts with a private firm to provide transportation and, like Lowell, must pay a substantial portion of the costs itself. Montclair's transportation bill is $2.4 million a year, of which the state of New Jersey reimburses the district for $1.1 million. All elementary and secondary students who live 1¼ miles or more from their school (70 percent of Montclair's students) qualify for busing. Buses also drop off students after school to babysitters and private day care centers that are more than 1¼ miles from schools. Some parents choose schools far enough from home to ensure their children will qualify for busing. Other parents want a school that is close or convenient to their place of work. Still others are attracted by expanded day programs at the elementary schools. For an additional charge, these schools will provide child care from 7:30 AM until the regular school day begins and from the end of school until 5:30 PM. Some parents are influenced by the size or grade configuration of the school. Montclair has eight elementary schools that range in enrollment from 175 to 605 students. Two are pre-K-2 schools; one is a 3-5 school, another is a 3-5 program in a middle school, and four are pre-K-5 schools. The two middle schools enroll students in grades 6-8; one has an enrollment of 520 and the other an enrollment of 616.

The majority of parents in Montclair are influenced by the specialized programs and staffing at particular schools. All of the district's 10 elementary and middle schools are magnet schools. Each features a specialized theme or program designed to appeal to different student interests and abilities. Montclair's educated (40 percent of the community's residents have college degrees) middle- and upper-middle-class parents are serious and aggressive educational consumers. They shop around carefully before deciding which magnet program is best for their child. They are also capable of applying pressure on the assistant superintendent and superintendent to "ensure" their child gets a particular school or teacher. Administering "Freedom of Choice" requires intestinal fortitude and considerable political skill. The 10-year tenure of Montclair's superintendent, Dr. Mary Lee Fitzgerald, is evidence of both of these qualities.

MONTCLAIR'S MAGNET PROGRAMS

The eight elementary and two middle schools offer a variety of magnet themes or programs. The 10 magnet programs are Gifted and Talented (three schools), Science and Technology (two schools and one program), International Studies (one school), Fundamental (one school), Montessori (one school), and Family (one school).

Gifted and Talented

Gifted and Talented (G/T) was one of the two original magnets created in 1977. Today the G/T program is located in three schools (primary, intermediate, and middle) and is the linchpin of Montclair's desegregation effort. The three schools originally enrolled mostly minority students. With the introduction of the G/T program, the district made a commitment in plant, materials, and staff in order to attract white and middle-class students to the three schools. That commitment has resulted in success.

Nishuane

Nishuane is a pre-K–2 school in the south end of Montclair that enrolls 605 students, 54 percent of whom are white, 43 percent are black, and 3 percent are Asian or Hispanic. The philosophy at Nishuane and the other two G/T schools is that all children are gifted. It is the school's responsibility to identify, nurture, and develop individual talents or gifts of children. Nishuane has no admission requirements beyond the criteria used in the district's "Freedom of Choice" plan and enrolls special-needs students, as do all of Montclair's schools. Students and their parents select schools, like Nishuane, based upon interest.

Nishuane is divided into five houses of 125 students each. Houses A and B consist of grades pre-K and K; houses C, D, and E comprise grades 1 and 2. Within each house students take their core academic classes in self-contained classrooms taught by a single teacher. Each house offers G/T elective classes for its students that are taught by a variety of teachers.

Three fourths of each day is taken up with daily instruction in core subjects (language arts/reading, math, science, social studies) and weekly instruction in related arts subjects (music, art, physical education/family life, library). Two afternoons a week, from 2:00 to 3:00 PM, students are enrolled in their G/T elective classes. Two weekly electives, one on Tuesdays and one on Wednesdays, are taken for a 3-month period beginning in October. Students begin a second cycle of two new electives from January to March, and a third cycle of electives from March to May. Because of their young age and immaturity, prekindergarten and kindergarten students are not allowed to take electives until the second and third cycles, respectively.

Students may choose from more than 60 G/T elective classes (20 each trimester) offered at Nishuane. Sign-up sheets are sent home with students and must be signed and returned by their parents. The electives are divided into Aesthetics and Creative I offerings. Aesthetics are open to all children and are based upon student interest. In language arts the offerings include "Language Lingo," "Tell Me a Story," and "Radio Radio"; in math, "From Soup to Nuts," "Relationshapes," and "Mind Benders"; in science, "Green Thumb Gang," "Kitchen Chemistry," and "Solar System"; in social studies, "Cafe International," "Exploring Your Community," and "It's a Camper's World"; in music, "Lift Every Voice," "Strike up the Band," and "Piano"; in performing arts, "Playacting" and "Playwriting"; in physical arts, "Gymnastics" and "Sport Skills"; and in visual arts classes include "The World of Machines," "Puppet Showcase," and "Clay."

Creative I classes provide enrichment for students who have special abilities or talents in a specific area. Students must be nominated and selected for Creative I classes. Typically, parents do the nominating and teachers and the principal do the selecting. A screening process with predetermined criteria is used to determine eligibility for each Creative I class. In language arts, students must be reading at least 1 year above grade level. In math, students must understand patterns, place value, graphing, and word problems and be able to compute with one- and two-digit numbers. In social studies and science, students must demonstrate knowledge of basic concepts and indicate knowledge and creativity in answering a set of 10 basic social-studies or science questions. In art, student age, interpretation, and creativity are evaluated in the areas of drawing, painting, sculpture, clay, and design. In "Danastics," students' gymnastic ability is evaluated in terms of flexibility, endurance, rhythm, coordination, and flow of movement. In chorus, students must demonstrate ability in singing, echo clapping, musical flash cards, and musical intervals.

Competition to be selected for Creative I classes is stiff, and individual parents are not above lobbying teachers and the principal long and hard for their child's inclusion. Children of less aggressive parents are at a disadvantage because the nominating process for Creative I is parent driven. As a result, resegregation by social class and race takes place within the school because lower-income and minority students are underrepresented in the Creative I classes. Teachers and the principal at Nishuane are aware of this problem and identify and support students with abilities and talents who do not have parental support. The school also established a goal of having every student in at least one Creative I class by the 1991–92 school year.

Nishuane has excellent facilities and staff that make a high-quality G/T program possible. The school has a dance studio, a large auditorium with stage, two music rooms, and two art rooms. The staff includes a half-time drama teacher, two music teachers, two art teachers, and two physical education teachers. One of the physical education teachers is skilled in gymnastics, and the other is skilled in dance.

Besides providing instruction in related arts subjects, Aesthetics and Creative I, these specialty teachers also assist with the annual stage productions put on by the five houses. Each house performs a major musical play once a year. The drama teacher writes the script, the music teachers compose the songs, and the art teachers make the scenery for each production. Students help the teachers in each of the three areas and of course sing, dance, and act in the productions.

Additional features at Nishuane include foreign language classes for students in grades K–2. Two full-time teachers offer classes in French and Spanish 4 days a week to interested and qualified students. Nishuane also has an Exploritorium, which is a large room of science-related materials organized into learning centers. Core academic teachers may take their class periodically to the Exploritorium to work with manipulatives in three centers on plants, fossils, and the senses. There is also an aquarium for the study of fish. The Exploritorium also doubles as the Creative I science classroom.

At the completion of grade 2, students must transfer to an elementary school. Nishuane students are guaranteed admission to Hillside, which is the elementary G/T school. Families choosing Hillside do not need to go through the centralized application and selection process again. More than 90 percent of the students continue the G/T program at Hillside. Students wishing to transfer to a different school go through the "Freedom of Choice" application and transfer process at the central office.

Hillside

Hillside is a 3–5 school of 600 students located across the street from the school district's central office in west central Montclair. Fifty-one percent of Hillside's students are white, 44 percent are black, and 5 percent are either Asian or Hispanic. The school day is from 9:05 AM to 3:30 PM and is divided into eight periods. Students spend four periods in academic core classes (language arts, social studies, math, science), one period in related arts (music, art, library, PE/family life), one period in lunch, and two periods in G/T electives.

Students have two core teachers, one for language arts/social studies, and one for math/science. Students are instructed in 2-hour blocks by each of the two core teachers. Fifty students are paired with a language arts/social studies teacher and a math/science teacher for the school year. The two core teachers have selected each other and work together as a team.

As at Nishuane, the G/T electives are divided into Aesthetics and Creative I classes. Aesthetics are open to all students and include more than 200 electives. A sampling of course titles, follows. In language arts, "Young Authors," "Public Speaking," and "Journalism"; in math, "Mathemagic," "Checkmate," "Computer Programming"; in science, "Electricity (AC/DC)," "Curious Creatures," and "Weather Study"; in social studies, "The Wild West: Cowboys, Cowgirls, and Indians," "Philosophy and Logic," and "Afro-American/Woman Studies"; in vocational arts, "Introduction to Typing," "Zig and Zag," and "The World of Plastics"; in dance/drama, "Ballet I," "Jazz Tap," "Clowns Character and Makeup," and "Scene Study and Performance"; in art/music, "Sing-A-Long," "Orchestra," "Musical Grab Bag," "Crafts," and "Fine Arts."

Creative I classes are competitive and open only to students who have been nominated and selected. Hillside's screening process for admission to Creative I classes is similar to Nishuane's but also includes the use of students' norm-referenced test scores. Students who qualified for Creative I classes at Nishuane may continue in the same Creative I classes at Hillside. Some of the Creative I offerings in language arts include "A Study of the Classics" and "Creative Writing"; in math, "Math Olympiad" and "Introduction to Algebra";

in science, "Chemistry" and "Study of Light"; and in social studies, "World History" and "Early Village and City Life."

Students sign up for six Aesthetics/Creative I classes to be taken during their two elective periods each day. In order to fit six electives into two periods, Hillside operates "A" and "B" day scheduling. Three consecutive "A" days (Monday, Tuesday, Wednesday) are followed by three consecutive "B" days (Thursday, Friday, and Monday of the next week. "A" days Tuesday, Wednesday, Thursday are followed by three consecutive "B" days on Friday, Monday, Tuesday, and so on through the year. The "A" and "B" day scheduling allows students to fit three Aesthetics/Creative I classes into each of the two elective periods on a weekly basis. Scheduling for Aesthetics and Creative I classes is done arena-style, classroom by classroom, three times a year. Students therefore end up taking a total of 18 electives during a school year.

The complicated and time-consuming process for signing up and scheduling the G/T electives miraculously works. Parents receive a choice sheet 2 weeks before scheduling and return it to the school with their preferences indicated. Most Aesthetics and Creative I classes enroll students from multiple grade levels, typically grades 3–4 or 4–5. Some enroll students in all three grades, and a few classes are limited to one grade level.

In addition to Aesthetics and Creative I offerings, students may take French or Spanish. Foreign language classes meet daily, so students enrolled have three instead of six Aesthetics and Creative I classes. Remedial electives are available for students who need extra time to acquire basic skills. Participation in the select Hillside Traveling Troupe is available to 4th and 5th graders with talent in those areas. Students must audition, and the competition is stiff. In 1990–91, 200 students tried out for the 30-member troupe of dancers and singers. The Troupe gives 11 or 12 performances a year in nursing homes, community centers, and public schools in New Jersey, New York, and Connecticut.

Students not selected for the troupe have opportunities to perform in drama and musical productions put on by the school. One major musical production is put on each year and is open to all who wish to perform. In 1990–91 the production was *It's Gotta Be Oz*. This 2-hour spectacular featured music from *The Wizard of Oz* and *The Wiz* and was performed by a cast that included seven Dorothys.

Like Nishuane, Hillside has the necessary staff and facilities to offer a high-quality G/T program. In addition to the academic core teachers, the school has two full-time teachers each in French, Spanish, and music, a full-time and a half-time teacher in art, one drama and one dance teacher, and half-time teachers in photography and gymnastics. Facilities include a large auditorium with stage, two music rooms, a dance studio, darkroom, fully equipped gymnastics area, and a science exhibit room similar to Nishuane's Exploritorium.

At the completion of the 5th grade, Hillside students transfer to one of the district's two middle schools. Between 85 and 90 percent choose Glenfield, which offers continuation of the G/T program. Hillside students are guaranteed admission to Glenfield. Students wishing to transfer to the other middle school must apply through the "Freedom of Choice" centralized admission procedure at the district office.

Glenfield

Glenfield is located in east central Montclair not far from Nishuane. It is the larger of the district's two middle schools, enrolling 616 students in grades 6–8. Forty-six percent of Glenfield's students are white, 50 percent are black, and 4 percent are either Asian or Hispanic.

Students are assigned to one of six houses. Each house has approximately 100 students and four teachers. The teachers provide instruction in the four core academic subjects of language arts, social studies, math, and science. Students have a choice between traditional and open houses. Traditional houses include students from only one grade level who are instructed separately in the four core academic classrooms. Open houses include students from all three grade levels, who are instructed using an interdisciplinary team-teaching approach.

Teachers in the open houses work cooperatively and attempt to make connections among the four core subjects through the use of themes. While the social studies teacher is discussing the Civil War, the language arts teacher is assigning students *The Red Badge of Courage,* and the math teacher is having students graph railway mileage of the North and South. Integrating all four core subjects is not an easy task and is not done with every unit or theme. Language arts and social studies provide the easier interconnections and the bulk of interdisciplinary team teaching opportunities. Because students are in their houses for at least two consecutive periods, and in some cases three, teachers in the open houses can arrange for large-group lectures and small-group discussions and other variations to deliver instruction. Students are heterogeneously grouped within each house. There is no tracking by ability in the core academic classes. However, students who have been identified as academically talented are given different assignments and additional work to do within their core classes, just as students are who have been identified as having academic difficulties.

The school day begins at 8:00 AM and ends at 2:19 PM and is divided into eight periods. There is also a zero period before school officially opens, for a total of nine periods for some students. Four periods each day are devoted to the core academic subjects, with a fifth period for lunch. That leaves three periods a day for G/T electives in either Aesthetics or Creative I.

One of the three electives must be in PE/family life. Students have a variety of courses to choose from in this area. Selections include "Ballet," "Modern Dance," "Volleyball," "Ultimate Frisbee," "Gymnastics" (Aesthetics or Creative I), and "Universal Fitness." The two remaining elective periods—three if a student enrolls in the before-school zero period—are devoted to the many Aesthetics and Creative I offerings available to students.

Aesthetics and Creative I courses are offered in humanities, science, math, and arts. Examples of course offerings include "Literary Magazine," "Stock Market," "Time Was" (humanities); "Mix It Up," "Environmental Education," "Here's to Your Health" (science); "Introduction to Statistics," "Computers and Math," "Math Extravaganza" (math); "Orchestra," "Ceramics," "Cooking Around the World," and "Architectural Design" (arts).

The academic year is divided into quarters. Students sign up for Aesthetics and Creative I electives (with parental approval) four times a year. Students may also choose to take either French or Spanish during an elective period. Foreign language classes are offered at the introductory, intermediate, and advanced levels. Students who complete 3 years of advanced classes receive credit for 1 year of high school foreign language.

As with the other G/T schools, Glenfield has excellent facilities. The school has a dance studio; video area with cameras, editing machine, and graphics generator; a darkroom well stocked with photographic supplies; two music rooms with electronic keyboards, sequencers, and synthesizers; an art room with a Macintosh II; a large community auditorium with stage attached to the school; and a planetarium.

Glenfield sponsors a variety of student performances and productions. The school puts on four small dramatic plays annually, which are directed by the drama teacher and open to all students who wish to perform. The drama teacher also directs one large musical each year that students must audition for. In 1990–91 it was *Bye Bye Birdie*. The instrumental music teacher assists in the musical by training the pit orchestra, and the vocal music teacher oversees the soloists and chorus. Music students may audition for the three touring groups: orchestra, jazz ensemble, or chorus. The dance teacher organizes several holiday programs performed by interested students. These groups give several performances in and around the community each year.

Glenfield's G/T program is of the same high quality as Nishuane's and Hillside's. Together the three schools offer the most popular magnet program in the district and have made the desegregation of Montclair's public schools possible.

Science and Technology

Mt. Hebron

Mt. Hebron, the district's other middle school, is located in a middle-class neighborhood in north central Montclair. The school enrolls 520 students in grades 6–8, 42 percent of whom are white, 49 percent are black, and 9 percent are Asian or Hispanic. In 1977 a Fundamental magnet program was introduced at Mt. Hebron in order to attract minority students to the school. Although the magnet program was initially successful, it gradually lost popularity in the early 1980s. The Fundamental label became identified with remedial or basic education, and families were therefore reluctant to choose Mt. Hebron. In an effort to change the image and improve the attractiveness of the school, the district replaced the Fundamental magnet program with a Science and Technology program in 1985.

The Science and Technology program is designed to attract students who have an interest in science, technology, and computers. Numerous science electives and extensive computer applications are the main features of the magnet program. Although much of the organization of Mt. Hebron's program is similar to Glenfield's, there are differences. Like Glenfield, Mt. Hebron is organized into houses of 100 students and four teachers each. There are two 6th-grade and three 7th- and 8th-grade houses. The four teachers provide instruction in the core academic subjects of language arts, social studies, science, and math within self-contained classrooms. While Glenfield groups students heterogeneously within the core classes, Mt. Hebron provides separate advanced core classes in math and language arts for all three grades and in science for grades 7 and 8. Criteria for selection to advanced core classes include norm referenced test scores, student grades, and teacher recommendations.

The content of core classes at Mt. Hebron is identical to Glenfield's with the exception of 7th- and 8th-grade science. Students spend the second half of the year in these courses taking a specially designed thematic minicourse. The 7th-grade minicourses are "Forensics," "Investigating Terrestrial Ecosystems," and "Topics in Life Science." The 8th-grade courses are "Geology of New Jersey" and "Genetics." Students take only one minicourse each year, with the choice determined by their core science teacher.

Like Glenfield, Mt. Hebron's school day is divided into eight periods: four for core academic classes, one each for PE/family life and lunch, and two for electives. Students select two new electives each grading period for a total of eight electives a year. Electives are available in music, foreign languages (French and Spanish), art, and home economics. Science, technology, and computers constitute the majority of electives and include "Introduction to Technology," "Business Education/Keyboarding," "LEGO TC Logo," "Design and Problem Solving in Technology," "Tech I and II," "CAD," "Rocketry," "Voyage of the Mimi," "It's a MOD World," "Robotics," "Media-Video Lab," and "Industrial Technology."

All 6th graders take "Introduction to Technology" and "Business Education/Keyboarding," which teach keyboarding and related computer skills. Core classes make extensive use of computers. Research projects are assigned each grading period, and students are expected to use computers in preparing their projects. Science and technology electives at grades 7 and 8 incorporate computer-related skills in their daily lessons and activities.

Mt. Hebron has the most extensive computer facilities of any magnet school in Montclair. Three large labs and five minilabs provide considerable computer access for students. The largest laboratory consists of 25 IBM PC computers and is used primarily for the "Introduction to Technology" course. A Laser Lab with 12 Apple II E clones is where the "Business Education/Keyboarding" course is taught, and a Macintosh lab equipped with 12 Mac Plus computers is used for graphics instruction. In addition, minilabs of three or four Apple II GS computers are located in each of the five houses. A file server connects all labs to each other and makes schoolwide operation possible with single software programs.

Computers are used extensively in remediation as well as in core and elective coursework. The IBM lab has a complete Josten's Learning Program software package for students who need additional individualized work in their core subjects. A well-equipped media center provides reference material to students through a CD-ROM and laser disks.

The science and technology emphasis is further developed through field trips and related activities. Field trips are taken to the Franklin Institute in Philadelphia, the Museum of Natural History and the Bronx Zoo in New York City, and Bear Mountain Environmental Center in West Point, New York. The latter is a 3-day camping experience. Related activities include the Mathematics Olympiad, the annual science and technology fair, and the science fair.

The Science and Technology program has been successful in attracting students and reinvigorating Mt. Hebron. Between 1988–89 and 1990–91 enrollment at Mt. Hebron grew by 10 percent, while enrollment at Glenfield increased by 7 percent. To some, Mt. Hebron still stands in Glenfield's shadow, but the shadow has become considerably smaller.

Magnet for Information Technology

The Magnet for Information Technology (MIT) is the result of a committee of parents and teachers who were charged with developing a net magnet program. MIT opened in 1990–91 with 75 students in grades 3–5, three teachers, and one secretary in a remodeled wing at Mt. Hebron. To ensure the new magnet's initial success, the district recruited two popular teachers with strong parent followings from Hillside and Edgemont schools and hired a third teacher with computer expertise to staff the program.

The MIT features team teaching, cross-grade grouping, interdisciplinary thematic curriculum, and computer application. Students are grouped heterogeneously into three flexible cross-grade classes or bytes, as they are called. After a 30-minute homeroom period, the bytes rotate among the three teachers during a 2¼-hour block of time for instruction in math, reading/language arts, and social studies/technology. Although most of the instruction takes place in the bytes, teachers periodically group 3rd, 4th, or 5th graders together for instruction on material specific to their grade level.

Students complete their morning schedule with 45 minutes of PE/family life classes, followed by lunch and recess. During the 1½-hour block in the afternoon, students return to their bytes for instruction from one teacher in either reading/language arts, math, or social studies/technology. Bytes have a different teacher and subject on Monday, Wednesday, and Friday. On Tuesday and Thursday afternoons, students work on individual and group projects related to the thematic curriculum being studied. At the completion of the afternoon block, students return to their bytes for a 20-minute homeroom period before going home.

The curriculum is thematic. In 1990–91 there were four themes: "Connections," "Big Blue Marble," "Inventions," and "Simulation Technology." Teachers attempt to relate some of their morning and Monday, Wednesday, and Friday afternoon lessons to a theme. The Tuesday and Thursday afternoon project sessions are entirely thematic.

Visitors to the MIT will not see much large-class, teacher-directed instruction. Minilessons by teachers are followed by individual or group work by students. Reading instruction is done through trade books and anthologies rather than basal texts. Students are taught writing skills through work on their projects and reports. Math is taught primarily with manipulatives. Students use carrots for measurement, Jell-O for shapes, and pumpkin seeds for estimating. Social studies consists largely of district-mandated map skills and the geography of New Jersey and the United States, but these are taught primarily through computer graphic applications.

All three teachers are computer literate and possess considerable audiovisual knowledge. A lab of 12 Apple II GS and 6 IBM PC computers is located in the social studies/technology room, and 4 Apple II GS computers are located in the math and language arts/reading rooms. Students learn primitive word processing, LOGO, data base, spread sheets, and graphics.

The MIT has had to undergo the typical growing pains of new programs. Some books and materials were slow to arrive initially, so teachers had to improvise at the beginning of the year. Developing the curricular themes has demanded considerable teacher time, effort, and sacrifice. Finally, the adjustment of the three teachers to each others' styles, strengths, and weaknesses has required patience and time. Parental enthusiasm for the MIT was high after the first year of operation. Enrollment was kept at 75, however, to allow refinement and improvement during the second year.

Watchung

Watchung is a pre-K–5 school in central Montclair that enrolls 440 students, 55 percent of whom are white, 40 percent are black, and 5 percent are either Asian or Hispanic. Watchung is the main feeder school for Mt. Hebron and the Science and Technology program. As with the MIT, the emphasis at Watchung is upon science and computer technology but with a more structured, teacher-directed approach. Special features of the school include a partnership with Rutgers University, projects with the National Aeronautics and Space Administration (NASA) and The National Geographic Society, and the offering of intersession courses.

Primary students (pre-K–2) are taught by individual teachers in self-contained classrooms. The curriculum incorporates a variety of science-related themes or topics throughout the year. Color, transportation, underwater creatures, and preservation of natural resources are examples of some of the themes. Computer experience for primary students is rather limited. Students make use of software programs in language arts, social studies, and math on the two Apple II GS computers in each classroom.

A science adjunct teacher from Rutgers University spends 2 days a week at Watchung working with primary students and teachers. His main responsibility is to introduce teachers to science materials and equipment they might not be familiar with and to assist teachers in the development of science units for use in their classrooms.

It is at the intermediate level (3–5) that the Science and Technology program becomes fully implemented. Intermediate students are team taught by two teachers, one of whom is responsible for language arts and social studies and the other for math and science. The thematic curricular approach begun in primary continues in grades 3–5. Students are introduced to a monthly theme such as weather, oceans, space, ecology, or electricity. Projects, experiments, and lab reports on each theme are assigned, and students work individually or in pairs to complete them.

Computer application is taught more extensively and systematically in grades 3–5. Minilabs of 8 to 10 Apple II GS and Macintosh computers are located at each of the three grade levels. Students learn basic programming and Microsoft Works. They also learn to do science and math simulations that relate to their projects.

Several special programs and partnerships enrich the intermediate Science and Technology curriculum. Students participate in a monthly NASA teleconference program that provides interactive lessons with NASA engineers on prearranged topics such as moon rocks, plants from space, and so forth. Watchung has also joined the National Geographic Society Kids Network. National Geographic Society assigns a topic, like acid rain, to a number of schools across the country. Students run experiments, collect data, and communicate the results to National Geographic via computer modems. National Geographic transcribes each school's results on computer disks and returns them so that students at the network schools can compare results.

Perhaps the most interesting special feature of Watchung's Science and Technology program is the intersession courses offered to intermediate students twice yearly. During the last week in January and the first week in May, the regular school schedule and curriculum are put on hold while students pursue an in-depth 2-day course on a topic of their choosing. Intersession courses are meant to be fun and emphasize problem solving and laboratory experiences. Some of the course titles include "Chemistry Laboratory," "Robotics," "Fly Me to the Moon," "Where the Wild Things Are," and "Flight, the Wild Blue Yonder."

The Science and Technology program has been successful in attracting students to Watchung. Like Mt. Hebron, Watchung had found its enrollment declining. With the introduction of the Science and Technology program, enrollment at Watchung increased 17 percent between 1988–89 and 1990–91, compared with an increase of 11 percent districtwide in the elementary grades.

Fundamental

Bradford Academy is a pre-K–5 school and is one of the original Fundamental magnets created in 1977. The magnet program was designed, in part, to attract minority students to the north end of Montclair, and it has been successful in accomplishing that goal. Of Bradford's 310 students, 43 percent are white, 52 percent are black, and 4 percent are Asian or Hispanic, giving it the highest percentage of black students of any elementary school in the district.

The Fundamental program emphasizes the basic core academic subjects of reading, math, science, and social studies, taught in a highly structured and disciplined environment. All classrooms are self-contained and teacher directed. Instruction is conducted in an orderly, step-by-step approach with extensive use of textbooks. Competition for good grades is encouraged and rewarded. Students receive report cards four times a year instead of two, as students in the other elementary schools do.

Parents wishing to enroll their children at Bradford must read and sign a statement in school philosophy and student conduct.

Student, parent, and teacher responsibilities are outlined in the statement, and all parties are expected to carry out those responsibilities. Considerable emphasis is placed upon appropriate student conduct. Expectations for student behavior in classrooms, hallways, restrooms, the lunchroom, on the playground, and on the bus are listed in detail. The discipline procedure for misbehaving students is also included.

Special features of Bradford include character education, a Junior Great Books program, and a large and well-stocked library and computer lab. Weekly lessons in character education are presented to students. Topics such as "Friendship," "Citizenship," "Respect," "Care of Property," "Sharing," "Kindness," "Positive Thinking," and "Cultural Differences" are discussed in class and reinforced schoolwide. Bradford's large library (largest of the eight elementary schools) is the location of the school's Junior Great Books program. Junior Great Books is an accelerated reading program for students in the upper quartile in grades 2–5. Students meet weekly in small groups with the school librarian to discuss assigned books. A large Apple lab with 28 II GS computers is the center for both student enrichment and remedial work. The lab has the Jostens Learning Program software, so students may work individually at their own pace on assigned and independent work.

The special features of Bradford's Fundamental program are not as impressive as those of the G/T or the Science and Technology programs. Bradford does not have the novel or highly visible activities that attract parent attention and support. The Back to Basics curriculum, so appealing in the mid-1970s, is less attractive in the 1990s. There is also the perception, accurate or not, that Bradford attracts slower students and less effective teachers than do the other elementary schools.

Recognizing the need for some changes, the district renamed the school Bradford Academy in 1990 to give it a newer and more appealing image. In the eyes of some, *academy* connotes an academic and selective school. Bradford's new image did not extend past its new name, however, and the Fundamental program has remained virtually unchanged. As a result, the school is having difficulty attracting students. Bradford has the lowest enrollment of the six original elementary schools. Its 1990–91 enrollment of 310 represented a 6 percent decline since 1988–89. In addition, Bradford's white enrollment of 43 percent is the lowest of any elementary school.

International Studies

Northeast is a pre-K-5 school of 329 students located in the northeast area of Montclair. Forty-four percent of its students are white, 39 percent are black, and 17 percent are either Asian or Hispanic. Northeast has the highest percentage of Asian and Hispanic students of any elementary school because the district's English-as-a-Second-Language (ESL) program is located at the school. Approximately 40 students from 19 countries, speaking 13 languages, are enrolled at Northeast. Most of these foreign-born students have professional parents who have been transferred to the United States for business reasons.

Students needing ESL instruction are tested upon admittance to Northeast. Depending upon the results of the admission tests, students receive ESL instruction once or twice a week. Students are placed into one of two age groups, Pre-K-K or 1-5, for instruction. Students are pulled out of their regular classroom, usually during reading/language arts, for 30 minutes of ESL instruction. End-of-the-year test results determine whether students exit or remain in the ESL program for another year. Students typically spend from 1-3 years in the program.

The International Studies program at Northeast is a natural extension and elaboration of the school's ESL program. International Studies emphasizes cultural awareness, foreign language instruction, and global studies. Students are taught in self-contained classrooms at each grade level. Two teachers, one for language arts/reading and one for math/science, provide instruction to each class. All students take Spanish as a foreign language. Pre-K-2 students receive instruction once a week; students in grade 3-5 receive daily instruction.

A yearly theme and related activities comprise the heart of the International Studies program. In 1990-91 the theme was "We Are the World." Holidays served to focus attention on a variety of countries and cultural practices: Columbus Day—Italy and Spain; Halloween—Guy Fawkes Day; Thanksgiving—England; Christmas/Hanukkah—religious practices around the world; Martin Luther King Day—Africa; St. Patrick's Day—Ireland; and May Day—traditional activities around the world.

In addition to holidays, schoolwide assemblies and festivals introduce students to the variety of art and music found in other cultures. Traveling art displays from the Soviet Union and Bali, as well as a cultural artifacts display from the Newark (NJ) Museum, made stops at Northeast during the 1990–91 school year. Culture Day and the Spring International Festival are annual programs at Northeast. Culture Day features dances, song, and costumes of various countries. The Spring International Festival features foods and games from around the world. The weekly music and art classes feature songs and projects from other countries.

Although the cultural awareness and foreign language components of the International Studies program are healthy, the global studies component is not. A few years ago the district provided inservice training in global education for a number of Northeast teachers. Unfortunately, most have since transferred to other schools, taking with them their expertise. The unimplemented curriculum combined with a turnover in teachers and principals has created some uncertainty at the school. Like Bradford, Northeast has had difficulty attracting students in recent years. Its 1990–91 enrollment of 329 represented a 6 percent decline from 1988–89.

Montessori

Edgemont is a pre-K–5 school of 314 students located in central Montclair. Fifty-two percent of the students are white, 43 percent are black, and 5 percent are either Asian or Hispanic. Originally designed to be an Arts Basic magnet, Edgemont, like Bradford and Northeast, found its program losing appeal and enrollment in the mid-1980s.

At the same time Edgemont was experiencing problems, a group of Montclair parents was lobbying for a Montessori option in the schools. Seeing an opportunity to satisfy parents and revive Edgemont's fortunes, the district introduced two pre-K–K Montessori classrooms to the school in 1987–88. Initially, the Montessori option was offered to complement the Arts Basic program. However, the option proved so popular that it replaced the Arts Basic program entirely. Two pre-K–1 and three pre-K–2 classrooms were added in 1988–89 and in 1989–90. Three more classrooms in 1990–91 brought the total to 10, of which four were pre-K–K, two were K–1, and four 1–3. By 1994 Edgemont will have 14 Montessori classrooms enrolling students from pre-K–6.

The Montessori philosophy or method was developed by Maria Montessori, an Italian physician, who believed children learned primarily through self-motivation rather than by teacher compulsion. In order to foster self-motivation, Montessori advocated freedom within a "prepared environment." Montessori classrooms feature an abundance of manipulatives such as pouring containers, cleaning materials, color tablets, cylinder blocks, sandpaper letters, metal insets, beads, bells, and maps. Students interact with these objects individually and with other children under teacher encouragement and direction. Children move freely about the classroom and may talk with other students as long as they are not disruptive. The classroom atmosphere is noncompetitive; students proceed at their own individual rate.

The Montessori philosophy does not appeal to everyone. To make sure the Montessori program at Edgemont did not serve a limited student clientele, the district aggressively recruited students from all of Montclair. Local day care, nursery, and Headstart programs were visited by district personnel. A slide presentation was developed to inform parents about the Montessori philosophy. Saturday open houses were held at Edgemont so prospective parents could inspect the school and talk with teachers.

Starting a Montessori program is an expensive undertaking. Each converted classroom required an investment of approximately $12,000 in manipulatives and other materials. New teachers had to be hired who possessed both New Jersey certification and an American Montessori certificate. Most of Edgemont's teachers had to be recruited from private Montessori schools in the local area. A few district teachers have been trained by a consultant from the American Montessori Society.

The school day at Edgemont begins at 8:30 AM and ends at 2:50 PM. A typical daily classroom schedule is as follows:

8:30–9:00	Arrival
9:00–9:30	Circle Time
9:30–10:15	Art, Music, Gym, or Library
10:15–11:30	Individual Work
11:30–12:15	Lunch
12:15–1:00	Rest
1:00–2:30	Individual Work, Sharing, Guests
2:30–2:50	Recess
2:50	Dismissal

In addition to the Montessori program, Edgemont has maintained two features of the Arts Basic Curriculum. The first is an Orff music program. All students have two 40-minute music classes during which they learn the fundamentals of music using speech, movement, and memory. Students typically begin with a familiar nursery rhyme they have memorized. They develop a rhythm for the rhyme and transfer it to a rhythm instrument such as a xylophone, glockenspiel, or timpani. Students compose a song using the pentatonic scale. The scale is made up of five notes and has no dissonance. Most anything played on the scale sounds good. Finally, body movements are added to complete the student composition.

The second feature is a Lincoln Center Arts-in-Education program. The program is a joint venture of Lincoln Center and Teachers College, Columbia University. For $6,000 a year selected teachers at Edgemont receive a 3-week summer workshop to learn how to infuse the arts into their classrooms. During the year professional performance groups and artists-in-residence visit the school. In 1990–91 members of the New York City Ballet presented *Four by Balanchine*; musicians from the Juilliard School of Music performed *Piano Focus and Friends*; and actors from Dearknows Theatre staged *Alice in Wonderland*.

The combination of arts and Montessori has given Edgemont a strong magnet program with considerable appeal. Enrollment increased 5 percent from 1988–89 to 1990–91. The increase would have been even greater, but when a popular teacher was transferred from Edgemont in 1990 to get the MIT program started at Mt. Hebron, a number of students followed her.

Family

Montclair's newest magnet program (along with MIT) is located at the former Rand Elementary School in east central Montclair. In recent years the school had been part of a three-building high school complex. The school was completely renovated in 1990 and reopened in 1990–91 as Rand Family Magnet. One hundred seventy-five pre-K–2 students attend Rand. Fifty-seven percent are white, 37 percent are black, and 6 percent are either Asian or Hispanic.

Rand Family Magnet is the product of a committee of parents and teachers charged by Montclair's superintendent to develop a new magnet program for the district. Approximately 30 parents and several teachers first met in September, 1989 to discuss ideas for a magnet program. During the fall of 1989 members of the committee visited a variety of magnet schools in the East and Midwest. The district gave teachers release time and paid for committee members' travel expenses.

Although the committee had no model firmly in mind, museum and environmental programs were among the early favorites. In the course of their visitations committee members came across a family magnet school that appealed to almost everyone. The committee put together its proposal for such a school in January and presented it to the school board in February. The board approved the proposal, and interested teachers and a principal were identified, interviewed, and hired by the end of March. Seven teachers and the principal began planning in April, and Rand Family Magnet opened its doors in September, 1990.

Rand Family Magnet is a primary school that features family involvement, nongraded classes, and an emphasis upon nature and the environment. Rand welcomes participation of parents and other family members. In fact, a requirement for admission to the program is that one member of each student's family must be committed to regular involvement with the school. That regular involvement may be volunteering in classrooms, assisting in workshops, or contributing to fund-raising projects. Teachers at Rand are expected to encourage parent participation in their classrooms and have parent volunteers assisting them.

Family involvement is encouraged by the school's full-time family coordinator. She recruits parent volunteers for classrooms, guest lessons, field trips, and social events. She also organizes parent workshops on a variety of topics such as positive child behavior, parenting skills, fathers' group, and gender awareness. The coordinator, who has a degree in social work, also acts as a counselor for parents and children who are having difficulties.

A large family room serves as the central meeting place for parents and other family members at Rand. The room is furnished with a couple of cribs, some tables and easy chairs, and a stove and refrigerator. Fresh coffee and sweet rolls contribute to an inviting atmosphere. Parents assisting at the school may bring their younger children, who are watched by adults in the family room.

Self-contained nongraded classes and multi-age groupings allow students to progress at their own individual pace. There are four multi-age groupings at Rand: 4 and 5, 5 and 6, 6 and 7, and 4–6. The curriculum is developmental and thematic. Textbooks are not used. Math is taught through manipulatives and reading through literature. Themes, such as Habitats, Adaptations, and Cycles, focus on nature and the environment. Habitats include those of animals and humans. The classroom and home are treated as examples of habitats. Adaptations of plants and animals to their environment are discussed. Cycles, such as those of wind, water, and air are described, as well as the effects of pollution upon each.

The environmental emphasis was further developed in 1991–92 when a petting zoo, aquarium, and outdoor pond were added, and partnerships with the Montclair Recycling Center, Roseland Environmental Center, Turtle Back Zoo, and Newark and Morris Museums were underway.

It is a little early to declare Rand Family magnet a success, but if initial parent reaction is any indication, the school has a bright future. Parent interest led to the hiring of three additional teachers and an increased enrollment to 250 in 1991–92.

EVALUATING "FREEDOM OF CHOICE"

"Freedom of Choice" appears to be quite successful in promoting academic improvement, equity, and diversity. Evidence of academic improvement is found in a 1990 study conducted by Beatriz Clewell and Myra Joy for the Educational Testing Service (ETS). Clewell and Joy compared reading and math scores of students in grades 1 through 8 from 1984 (the year before "Freedom of Choice" was introduced) to 1988, and found they had risen substantially. Particularly noteworthy was the finding that test scores rose at all grade levels for minority as well as majority students.

Reading scores for white students in grade 1 went from the 80th to the 83rd percentile, in grade 2 from 79th to 85th, in grade 3 from 81st to 83rd, in grade 4 from 80th to 85th, in grade 5 from 78th to 81st, in grade 6 from 79th to 82nd, in grade 7, from 77th to 80th, and in grade 8 from 81st to 82nd. Math scores of white students in grade 1 went from the 79th to 81st percentile, in grade 2 from 81st to 89th, in grade 3 from 83rd to 86th, in grade 4 from 82nd to 91st, in grade 5 from 86th to 87th, in grade 6 from 82nd to 88th, in grade 7 from 81st to 89th, and in grade 8 from 84th to 90th percentile.

Improvement in reading and math scores for minority students was even more pronounced. Reading scores for minority students in grade 1 went from the 60th to the 71st percentile, in grade 2 from 64th to 70th, in grade 3 from 53rd to 60th, in grade 4 from 53rd to 61st, in grade 5 from 51st to 53rd, in grade 6 from 45th to 61st, in grade 7 from 45th to 57th, and in grade 8 from 52nd to 58th. Math scores for minority students in grade 1 went from the 50th to 59th percentile, in grade 2 from 60th to 68th, in grade 3 from 61st to 64th, in grade 4 from 55th to 70th, in grade 5 from 63rd to 74th, in grade 6 from 51st to 82nd, in grade 7 from 52nd to 70th, and in grade 8 from 61st to 76th.

In addition to improved academic performance, Montclair has been able to achieve racial and ethnic balance in all of its schools. All 10 of the elementary and middle schools are within 10 percentage points plus or minus of the districtwide average of 48 percent white and 52 percent minority. Eight of the 10 are within 6 percentage points. The two most imbalanced, Watchung and Rand Family, are within 7 and 9 points, respectively. Montclair has made a conscious effort not only to racially balance its schools but to hire more minority teachers and administrative staff. Twenty-eight percent of the district's supervisors and administrators and 29 percent of its teachers and counselors are minority individuals.

Although Montclair's accomplishments in improving academic performance and achieving racial balance are impressive, it should be pointed out that the district operates under conditions that make racial balance and academic performance easier to achieve than in other school districts. Montclair is an affluent and highly educated community that is progressive in outlook and more receptive to equity goals than are less well-educated and less affluent communities. A substantial proportion of the minority population in Montclair is professional and well educated, so the gap between majority and minority parents is not as great as it is in other communities. Montclair's relatively small population and geographic size contribute to a greater sense of community than may be found in larger cities. Because of its affluence and progressiveness, Montclair is able and willing to make the necessary financial commitment to ensure high-quality specialized programs that are attractive to parents and students. According to Montclair's business manager magnets cost the district 8.4 percent more than traditional programs in the schools would cost. The ability and the willingness of the district to spend the additional monies have resulted in diverse themes and specialty programs of very high quality.

Although "Freedom of Choice" does operate with some built-in advantages, its success has also been the result of careful collaborative planning. Montclair has developed its magnet schools gradually over a period of 14 years. The first magnets were introduced in 1977 and the two most recent in 1990–91. In 1985, 8 years after the first magnet school, the district undertook "Freedom of Choice." Montclair has taken its time implementing districtwide school choice.

Successful systemwide school choice requires support not just from administrators at the top but from teachers and parents as well. Montclair's administration has encouraged the participation of teachers in the development and implementation of magnet programs. While most magnet themes have been conceived administratively, the development and implementation of the themes has typically been left to teachers and principals. Three magnets, MIT, Montessori, and Family, were the inspiration of parents and teachers, not administrators.

Careful planning, adequate time, and teacher and parent participation do not always guarantee perfect programs, however. The Fundamental program at Bradford and the International Studies program at Northeast are in need of improvement. Magnets can lose their vitality and appeal and may need to be revived or replaced periodically. This happened at Mt. Hebron, Watchung, and Edgemont. Facilitating programmatic improvement in Montclair is the superintendent's ability to transfer teachers and principals to and from schools that are in need of change. In Montclair, unlike Lowell, principals serve at the pleasure of the superintendent, not of the school board.

Montclair has made use of collaborative planning, adequate time, and sufficient resources to transform all of its schools into magnets to be selected by parents through intradistrict "controlled" choice. The results have been impressive: improved academic achievement, increased racial and ethnic desegregation, and a variety of high-quality thematic and specialized programs.

Does Montclair's experience and the experiences of Richmond and Lowell with intradistrict choice hold any promise for improving public education? We think so, but as we saw in the Richmond experiment, the introduction of choice can result in failure as well as success. In Chapter 6 we will outline a step-by-step planning process for the successful implementation of systemwide choice.

CHAPTER SIX

Planning for Systemwide Choice

Planning and implementing systemwide choice requires sufficient resources, adequate time, and the support of parents, teachers, and administrators. Plans that are inadequately funded, hastily implemented, or autocratically conceived stand little chance of survival and long-term success. Successful planning of systemwide choice requires that parents, professionals, older students—indeed, the entire community—be full participants in a communitywide educational reform and renewal process.

A systemwide choice plan should be developed with more than just desegregation and parental and school professional satisfaction in mind, although desegregation and satisfied parents and school professionals will be among the results of a successful systemwide choice plan. The communitywide effort should have as its final goal the provision of systemwide school improvement. If everyone understands and accepts this basic commitment, planning will be much easier and much more successful.

In this chapter we describe a step-by-step planning process for implementing systemwide choice, specifically the combination of alternative or magnet schools and programs and "controlled" choice. The planning process we describe is based upon the actual experiences of school districts that have successfully implemented systemwide "controlled" choice plans. The planning process can be divided into four distinct phases, which are outlined as follows:

Phase I: Mechanisms for Initial Planning
    Build a Constituency
    Create a Citywide Parent/Professional/Community Council
    Conduct Parent/Professional Surveys

Phase II: Development of a "Controlled" Choice Plan
    Develop a Student Assignment Policy
    Design a "Controlled" Choice Plan
    Create a Parent Information System

Phase III: *Planning Individual Alternatives or Magnets*
    Establish Individual School Planning Teams
    Develop an Individual School Plan

Phase IV: *Implementation*
    Inform the Community
    Assign Staff and Students to Alternatives or Magnets

PHASE I: MECHANISMS FOR INITIAL PLANNING

Build a Constituency

The first and most important step in developing mechanisms for initial planning is to build a constituency for choice. Building a constituency means gradually and patiently working with parents, teachers, administrators, and school board members to make sure everyone has a general understanding of the concept of choice in public education and how it can improve the education offered in all of the district's schools. Depending upon the initial interest in and knowledge about alternative and magnet schools and programs and "controlled" choice among community members, Phase I may take from 6 months to a year.

As the community considers the possibilities and problems in instituting choice options and plans, some people will become enthused about the concept while others will reject it out of hand. Thus the development of mechanisms for exploration, information gathering, and information dissemination are crucial and must be conducted with great care and patience or the entire planning process will suffer.

The proposed introduction of choice is a major change and is likely to make everyone a bit nervous, even frightened. Choice options and plans like alternative and magnet schools and programs and "controlled" choice undermine or eliminate traditional practices such as guaranteed attendance at neighborhood schools, administrative imposition of districtwide curricula, and teacher seniority in instructional and building assignments. If these traditional practices are to be changed successfully, it is essential that the planning process be conducted in a democratic and collaborative fashion. Everyone must be given a chance to voice concerns and have them discussed in a fair and understanding manner.

One group frequently overlooked when developing a constituency is that of parents who do not have children presently in the public school system. This includes parents of preschool children, parents of children who attend private schools, and parents whose children are beyond school age. All of these parents are voters and taxpayers, and their support will be essential if adequate funding is to be provided for the implementation of choice. In addition, community organizations, social agencies, the business community, and the local political structure need to be informed and brought into the planning process to ensure broad-based support for reform.

A second group frequently overlooked is that of minority parents, especially those who do not speak English. Great care must be taken to ensure that *all* parents, especially those who are not English speaking, are contacted and included in the initial planning process. Mechanisms such as citywide parent planning councils, parent surveys conducted in a variety of languages, and informational meetings in minority neighborhoods are particularly effective and will be discussed later in greater detail.

Care must be taken to ensure that teachers and principals also have a prominent role in the planning process. Choice must not be seen by teachers and principals as benefiting only parents and students. Choice must also contribute to greater professional status and satisfaction and improved working conditions for teachers and principals if they are expected to support it. After all, the primary responsibility for delivering specialized programs and administrating "controlled" choice falls on the shoulders of teachers and principals. The success of any choice plan ultimately rests with the professional staff.

Once the process of building a constituency has begun, the next step is to conduct a feasibility study to see if there is sufficient communitywide support to pursue the choice plan further. A list of questions needs to be developed and answered: Do parents want to be able to choose the schools their children attend? If so, are they willing to give up the concept of neighborhood schools? Do principals and teachers want to be able to choose the kind of instructional and curricular program they can offer? If so, are they willing to transfer voluntarily to new buildings to practice the kind of schooling both they and parents want? What specific kinds of alternatives and magnets do parents, teachers, and principals want the school district to create? Are there teachers interested and capable of delivering the kinds of specialized programs indicated by parents? Are parents willing to have their children transported by bus in order to attend the school of their choice? Finally, how much is the choice plan expected to cost, and is the community willing and able to make the financial commitment to implement it? Getting the answers to these and other questions requires systematic gathering of community opinion. An excellent way to go about this is the creation of a citywide parent/professional/community planning council.

Create a Citywide Parent/Professional/Community Council

The citywide council should be made up of at least one parent representative elected by the parents and a teacher representative elected by the teachers from each school in the district. Interested principals should be asked to join the council and should also be represented by a delegate chosen by their professional association. Other council members should include representatives from the business community, social service agencies, and community organizations.

The first task of the council is to investigate and collect data on what other school districts have done to create alternative or magnet schools and programs and implement "controlled" choice plans. Descriptions of successful alternatives and magnets and "controlled" choice plans from around the country should be made available so council members can acquaint themselves with both. Ideally, teams of parents, teachers, and principals should visit selected school sites around the country to see choice in operation. Eventually the council will want to identify several different kinds of schools from very traditional to nontraditional and, perhaps, 5–10 themes or specialized programs it thinks parents and teachers in the district might be interested in. The range of specialized or thematic programs and schools should include the traditional as well as the more progressive, so that parents have a variety of educational and curricular options to choose from. Needless to say, options such as religious schools or racially exclusive academies, which violate state and federal laws, will not be considered.

When council members have identified the range of acceptable possibilities they think will be of interest, they should become involved in explaining these options to other parents, teachers, and the community at large. The council will want to keep the local communications media—including newspapers, television stations, and access channels of local cable companies—informed of its activities and plans. In addition, all council meetings should be open to the public and the media.

Conduct Parent/Professional Surveys

After the initial data collection and identification of possible options, the council should conduct districtwide parent/professional surveys to determine the degree of demand for each of the specialized options and the level of support for "controlled" choice. The parent survey form (see Appendix A for an example of a parent survey) contains a limited number of forced-choice questions. One question asks parents to indicate their preferences from the list of 5–10 specialized options. Another asks about parents' willingness to have their children attend school outside their neighborhood. Additional questions seek information on parent and student racial and ethnic background, how many children the parents are responding for, their grade level, and present school location.

The parent survey should be prepared in all appropriate languages and sent home with students, to be returned by them to their school. Experience indicates this approach ensures the highest response rate. Parent survey forms should also be distributed at all preschools and private schools and in public places like libraries and shopping malls to ensure a representative response. A rate of return is difficult to predict, but it is likely to be higher than expected. Worcester, Massachusetts experienced a return rate of 38 percent on its first parent survey, but saw it increase to 50 percent on its second, and 80 percent on its third as parents became more aware of and familiar with it.

The professional survey is administered simultaneously with the parent survey and contains the same forced-choice questions asked of parents. Teachers and principals indicate their preferences from the list of options. They are asked about their willingness to transfer voluntarily to a school with their preferred option. Teachers and principals also provide information about their racial/ethnic background, present school location, and teaching level (see Appendix B for an example of a professional survey). The returned parent/professional surveys are then forwarded to the district office for computer analysis. In entering the data into the computer, it is important that the parent responses be entered according to the number of children being responded for. A parent responding for three children is entered as three responses, not just as a single response. This enables survey analysts to compare the results directly with the total school population and/or with the district's school-age population.

After the data of the parent/professional surveys have been tabulated, the citywide parent/professional/community council meets to analyze and discuss the results. If it is determined that parents and/or teachers are not supportive of either "controlled" choice or alternative or magnet schools and programs, then some hard decisions must be made. One decision might be to offer a limited number of specialized programs rather than to transform all schools into alternatives or magnets. This is what Lowell decided to do initially. Another decision might be to institute an open enrollment plan that allows student transfers on a space-available basis while guaranteeing students admittance to their neighborhood school. A third decision might be to do nothing and keep things exactly as they are. If it is determined that parents and professionals are supportive of alternative or magnet schools and programs and "controlled" choice, the council is in a position to make a positive recommendation to the superintendent and school board to proceed with the planning and implementation of a systemwide plan.

PHASE II: DEVELOPMENT OF A "CONTROLLED" CHOICE PLAN

Develop a Student Assignment Policy

After completing the survey process and analyzing the results, district planners should devote the next 3–6 months to Phase II: The Development of a "Controlled" Choice Plan. The first step in developing a "controlled" choice plan is to establish a set of rules for student admission and transfers. The district must develop, and the school board must approve, a "controlled" admissions and transfer policy guaranteeing that all student assignments will conform to all civil-rights and desegregation requirements. The "controlled" admissions and transfer policy must:

- Ensure that every school in the district meets the desegregation standards set down by the courts and the U.S. Office of Civil Rights.
- Ensure that there are firm majority/minority quotas for each school in the district.

- Spell out the process by which parents make their choices. In most cases parents are asked to indicate first, second, and third preferences so that if their first choice is filled their children are automatically given a place in the second or third preferred school.
- Describe precisely how students are placed in schools by parent choice. In some districts seats are assigned on a first-come, first-served basis. In some districts seats are assigned by a computerized random selection process.
- Distinguish between the different kinds of parent choices and make clear the established arrangements for each kind: parents whose children are entering kindergarten, parents with older children who have just moved into the district or whose children have been attending private schools, and parents who wish to transfer their children from one school to another.
- State the policy on admission of siblings to alternatives or magnets. Some districts give preference to siblings of children in school.
- State whether children who live within walking distance of a school receive preference in admission to that school.
- Provide a fair and clearly understood appeals process so that parents who have been denied their first choice can petition for a review of the assignment decision (see Appendix C for an example of a "controlled" admissions and transfer policy).

Design a "Controlled" Choice Plan

After the parent/professional survey results have been tabulated and analyzed, district planners must determine which of the alternative or magnet schools and programs have the necessary parental and professional support for implementation. Planners must also decide how many of each alternative or magnet will be needed to satisfy demand. For example, if survey results indicated 40 percent of parents and teachers want a "back-to-basics" option, then approximately 40 percent of the alternatives or magnets ought to be "back-to-basics" options.

Once planners have developed a general picture of the range and number of specialized schools and programs to be offered, the next task is to determine how they will be distributed geographically throughout the district. For example, if that 40-percent figure for a "back-to-basics" option translates roughly into 10 schools, those 10 schools need to be dispersed throughout the district so as many children as possible can walk to them. This will of course lower transportation costs because fewer children will need to ride buses.

In small and midsized school districts, all alternatives or magnets can be districtwide schools to which students and their parents apply following the student assignment policy outlined earlier in the chapter. Large districts may want to group alternatives or magnets into several zones to save on transportation costs and make the assignment of students a manageable task. All attendance zones must be carefully drawn to replicate the majority/minority mix of the district as a whole so that the burden of integration and the opportunities for choice will be shared as equally as possible.

Create a Parent Information System

Central or zone parent information centers should be created to distribute information to parents and handle the registration of all students. This includes preschool and kindergarten students and all requests for transfer from one school to another. If all alternatives or magnets are districtwide schools, then the district needs only one parent information center. If the district has been divided into several attendance zones, then it will need a parent information center for each zone.

Parent information centers provide informational brochures in all appropriate languages. These brochures describe the alternative or magnet schools and programs parents may choose, state their location, and provide clear instructions on how parents can make their selections. Each center will need bilingual personnel fluent in the languages spoken by parents and a student assignment officer with a computer terminal connected to the central office's computerized system and student data base. The student data base should include complete records of all students and up-to-date information on the number and location of any and all available seats. The student assignment officer has the power to make school assignments on the spot, if parent choice and seat availability match up (see Appendix D for a design of a parent information center).

To ensure that all children have equal access to all available alternatives and magnets, the district needs to make a special effort to see that parents receive all the information they need to make informed choices. This means that all information prepared and distributed by the district must be in all appropriate languages. Informational brochures should be widely distributed not only at schools but at local churches, community organizations, and even supermarkets and shopping malls. Districts with the greatest success in reaching parents have parent liaisons or outreach workers who go into homes, churches, community centers, and social service agencies to meet and assist parents.

PHASE III: PLANNING INDIVIDUAL ALTERNATIVES OR MAGNETS

District planners must make sure that all of the alternatives or magnets requested by parents and the professional staff are actually created; that they are created in numbers to satisfy parental demand; and that they are distributed throughout the district based on the demographics of demand, the requirements of desegregation, and the need to keep transportation costs to a minimum. Planners must also decide whether an alternative or magnet school will be a district-wide or zone school.

Planners must ensure that each alternative or magnet school and program fits carefully into the district's "controlled" choice plan. The number of buildings necessary to house each of the specialized options must be determined, and the options must be assigned to particular buildings or to parts of buildings. In this process it is important to remember that a school is not necessarily an entire building. It is possible for a single large building to contain several specialized programs. Alternatives and magnets should be kept as small as possible, no larger than 400–500 students. This can be accomplished by subdividing a large building into smaller units.

Large districts with several attendance zones will need to ensure a representative mix of alternatives or magnets in each of the zones. Parents should be able to choose from among the same range of options whether they live in zone 1, 2, or 3. If planners decide to offer an alternative or magnet school or program at only one building site, then that alternative or magnet should become a district-wide school or program available to all families regardless of the attendance zone they live in.

Establish Individual School Planning Teams

Once the systemwide "controlled" choice plan has been adopted and the location of the alternatives or magnets decided, district planners must establish individual school or program planning teams for each alternative or magnet. These teams will spend the next 6 months planning the specialized theme or program to be offered at a particular school. The parent/professional surveys will provide the data needed to form the planning teams. For example, planning teams for the "back-to-basics" schools will be drawn from the principals, teachers, and parents who named that option as their first choice.

For elementary schools the planning team should include a principal, 3–5 teachers, and 6 parents. For middle and high schools the team should include a principal, 5–10 teachers, 10 parents, and 5 students. Teams can also include any other school or community people the other members feel would be useful. All members should be paid for their service on the team, because most of the planning will have to be done at after-school, evening, and summer sessions. To facilitate their task, teams should be provided with a list of goals to be achieved in the planning process. These goals are:

- To ensure that administrators, teachers, and parents of each school have a shared sense of mission and a clear understanding of and agreement about the distinctive program or programs their school is planning to offer, and knowledge of the steps necessary to conduct and complete the alternative or magnet school improvement process.
- To ensure that all segments of the school community, especially parents, are adequately involved in the process.
- To ensure that each school's planning process is complete, that is, that each school has considered all of the necessary elements involved in planning the specialized programs of their schools.
- To ensure that each individual school has followed every step of the planning process carefully and thoroughly.
- To enable each school to develop an evaluation process that is based on multiple outcome criteria.

In addition to a list of goals, individual school planning teams will also be given an explanatory document that deals with the following topics:

- What systemwide "controlled" choice is, what it is trying to accomplish, how it will work, and what it offers to both parents and professionals.
- What is the range of alternatives or magnets within the district.
- How the planning process in each school will be conducted.
- What elements, including a proposal for funding, must be in each school's plan.

- How additional people will be chosen to serve on the school planning team, if needed.
- What the timetable for completion of the planning team's work is.

Develop an Individual School Plan

The individual school plan will be structured by answers the planning team gives to questions from the six areas of educational philosophy, specialized program, school organization, proposed use of school facilities, descriptive brochure, and implementation timeline. A Schools of Choice/School Improvement Planning Form should be made available to assist the team (see Appendix E for an example of the form).

1. *Educational Philosophy*: The team should describe the school's educational philosophy, how this particular school proposes to serve that philosophy, what its distinctive approach to education will be, and how the school intends to improve the education offered to its parents and students. The philosophy should also include the school's program objectives for attracting parents and students and describe how it intends to meet the overall goal of desegregation.
2. *Specialized Curriculum*: The team must describe the school's specialized program, the subjects and time for each, and the expected outcomes in basic skills and other subjects. To aid the staff in learning new skills and subject areas, the plan should provide for continuing staff and program development. The role parents will play and how they will be kept informed of ongoing program development is a vital part of this process.
3. *School Organization*: The team should describe how the school will be organized and operated to carry out its shared sense of mission. This should flow clearly from the school's educational philosophy. A description of the school's organization should cover the following points:
   a. Governance structure: How major decisions are made; who will be involved in making them, including the role of teachers and parents.
   b. Grade structure and method of grouping, such as age-graded, flexible grouping by previous achievement, and mixed-age grouping.
   c. Scheduling: How the scheduling of classes will work within established state guidelines.

d. The integration of minority and female students in all classes, programs, and activities.

e. Reporting to parents: What kinds of changes, if any, will occur in standard reporting of progress; whether there will be regular parent conferences and open houses; what steps will be taken to ensure that limited-English-speaking parents understand how their children's progress is being measured and reported.

f. Behavior/discipline guidelines: How the school expects to discipline both student and staff misbehavior.

g. Parent involvement structure: How the school proposes to involve parents in its decision-making process and the operations of the school, including the role of the PTA, with special emphasis on how limited-English-speaking parents will be reached and involved.

h. Evaluation plan: How the school's specialized program will be evaluated. The evaluation plan should contain the goals and objectives for each component of the school's program. The school will specify the evaluation methods (such as achievement and attitude tests, attendance records, discipline referrals, and climate studies) that will be used to measure the success of the specialized program in achieving the stated goals.

4. *Proposed Use of the School's Facilities*: The team will outline the use of the assigned facilities and any needed alterations or additions.

5. *Descriptive Brochure*: Each planning team will prepare a succinct and readable description of its school. This will be used to inform parents and staff about the school's educational offerings.

6. *Implementation Plan*: How the school's plan will be implemented, including an implementation schedule; what additional staffing and other resources the school will need in order to get underway; and the source of the funding for such implementation.

PHASE IV: IMPLEMENTATION

Inform the Community

Implementation of the systemwide plan should begin in the spring prior to the opening of school in the fall. The first step in implementation is to distribute information about the plan to parents, professional staff, and other members of the community. This can be done by developing an informational booklet in all appropriate languages that covers the following points:

- The reasons for devising the plan: systemwide school improvement and educational excellence through parent and professional choice, desegregation, and the empowerment of parents and professionals to choose.
- The way the plan was developed: through active participation of parents, teachers, principals, students, and other members of the community.
- The range of specialized options available to parents and professional staff.
- The process of assigning students: the location of the parent information center(s) and other avenues of getting information, such as open houses and parent liaisons.
- The proposed means of financing the plan and a statement of its cost.
- The way parents make decisions about the alternative or magnets they want their children to attend.
- The system by which teachers and principals can make their choice of school assignment.

The booklet will also contain a form asking parents to indicate the first three school choices for each of their children for the opening of the school the following September. In addition, parents are asked to supply information about their children's ages, race and ethnicity, present school attended, and so on. The completed form should be mailed or delivered to the parent information center.

The informational booklet is a vital part of the campaign to acquaint parents and community members with the systemwide plan. Its preparation is the responsibility of the central administration. During Phase III, individual planning teams have already developed brochures describing the specialized programs at each of the alternatives or magnets. These brochures should be included in the informational booklet to give parents some idea of why they would want to enroll their children in a particular program or school.

The brochures and the booklet must be prepared in all appropriate languages and distributed to all parents in the district, as well as to parents of children in preschools and private schools. The booklet can be sent home with children and also be made available to visitors at schools and at parent information centers. The booklet should also be distributed to all teachers and principals so they will be fully informed when it is time to apply for teaching and administrative positions.

School staff should encourage parents to visit the parent information center(s) and any or all alternative or magnet schools or programs. Public information meetings should be scheduled at each school and at selected community locations. A telephone hotline can be established to handle questions from parents who are having difficulty making decisions. Finally, the systemwide plan should be publicized and described in as many different media outlets as possible including newspapers, television, and radio. A true "media blitz" should occur.

Assign Staff and Students to Alternatives or Magnets

During the time that the plan is being publicized, the teachers and principals will be making their choices of the alternative or magnet schools they wish to work in. The principals and teachers who volunteered to be members of the individual school planning teams will have first choice of positions in these schools. The assigned principal, the volunteer teachers, and the parents on the planning team of each alternative or magnet can act as a staff selection committee to review teacher applications and select the staff for the school. As teachers are selected by the team, they can volunteer to join the staff selection committee, if they choose.

It is hoped that all staff assignments can be based primarily upon teacher choices or teacher suitability for the specialized program, rather than upon seniority or administrative convenience. Because teacher contracts often prevent involuntary transfers, the central administration will need to work out an agreement with the teachers' union on how the rearrangement of school staff will occur. In any event, the staff assignment process should be scheduled so it can be completed by the end of the school year. That way, staffs of the new alternatives or magnets can spend the summer in curricular and instructional development activities.

As the parent choice forms come into the parent information center(s), the student assignment officer and staff have the job of sorting out the choices and matching them with the alternatives or magnets requested, the space available in the schools and programs, and the desegregation requirements of the "controlled" choice plan.

The first year will be the most difficult, in that every student is potentially up for assignment.

In any event, school systems must make the decision about the assignment of students and notify individual parents of their child's assignment before the end of the school year. That leaves the summer months for school personnel to respond to any parent appeals. Thus an appeal process must be identified and ready to put into place before student assignments are made.

The transportation of students will be a major undertaking for most districts. The difficulty and extra cost will depend on the current level of transportation provided by the district. In districts where most students walk to neighborhood schools, the implementation of systemwide choice will require a substantial increase in the amount of busing. Districts that are already busing large numbers of students will not be impacted as much.

An effective and cost-effective transportation system is a key ingredient in the success of any systemwide choice plan. It must not be seen as simply an add-on to the existing transportation system. Districts need to start from scratch, take into account all busing needs, and design a totally new transportation system. The best approach is to hire a transportation expert familiar with computer programs designed specifically for this purpose.

After students have been assigned to the schools and the staff selected, the newly assigned principal, staff, and parents of the school can spend the summer months beginning the translation of the planning team's design into appropriate organizational and classroom activities. The phrase "beginning the translation of the planning team's design" has been carefully and deliberately chosen. No one ought to expect a fully developed alternative or magnet school or program to spring from the minds of the district's planners or from a new staff on the first day of the school's official opening.

Some alternative or magnet schools and programs can be developed more quickly than others. For example, a "back-to-basics" option takes less time to put in place than a performing arts or microsociety option. Some alternatives or magnets, like Montessori, require specially trained and certified teachers. In these cases the district may not be able to start whole schools but may instead choose to begin with the lowest grade or grades and add a grade a year until the school is complete.

Whether certain alternatives or magnets take more or less time to develop, all of them must establish a collegial staff, provide staff development, put into place the new curriculum and school organization, establish a discipline code, create governance and parent-involvement structures, and develop a shared sense of mission.

Parents and staff should not expect schools and programs to be in their final, perfected form on opening day. It will take at least a year or two before all members of the school community—staff, parents, and students—become completely comfortable with the specialized program. Indeed, while implementing such a program it is important for parents and staff to remember that its development takes time. Meaningful school improvement does not come easily, nor does it come overnight.

CHAPTER SEVEN

The Future of Choice

We believe public school choice holds the key to improving public education in America. As Deborah Meier, noted East Harlem educator, points out, choice is "the necessary catalyst for the kind of dramatic restructuring that most agree is needed to produce a far better educated citizenry" (1991, p. 253). The case studies of Lowell, Montclair, and Richmond demonstrate the ability of properly conceived and implemented districtwide choice plans to deliver diverse educational programs that are equitable as well as excellent.

CHOICE: NECESSARY BUT NOT SUFFICIENT

Although public school choice can be the initial impetus for "dramatic restructuring," simply allowing parents to choose among whatever schools happen to exist in a public school system is not sufficient. Choice without a variety of high-quality and diverse options to choose from is a pseudo-innovation that produces little significant change. As the Lowell, Montclair, and Richmond examples clearly show, choice must be combined with genuine program diversity if meaningful school improvement is to take place. Choice must also allow teachers and principals to choose the kind of schooling they wish to practice and must provide the necessary individual school autonomy to make diversity possible. Choice must also include strong equity controls in order to make sure *all* students, but particularly poor and minority students, have equal access to everything a newly restructured school system has to offer. Finally, choice requires additional funding if it is to be successful.

Affluent districts like Montclair are fortunate because they are able to supplement state aid with local monies to offer choice programs of high quality. Less advantaged districts, like Lowell and Richmond, are heavily dependent upon state and federal funds for the development and implementation of their choice options. For a variety of reasons, Richmond now finds itself bankrupt. Lowell is currently struggling to keep its innovations alive and well in the face of severe budget cuts imposed by a recession in the Northeast. "Dramatic restructuring" thus requires a financial commitment not only from local school districts but from the state and federal governments as well.

If successful significant school improvement is going to happen in any public school district, it is not going to happen overnight, and it is not going to happen by school board or administrative command. There are too many school districts and states riding the tidal wave of choice with little thought to planning. Choice instituted in a hasty, ill-conceived, and top-down fashion is unlikely to be successful. As Richmond tragically learned, rushing into choice without adequate time for planning and the involvement of all members of the community can lead to educational and sometimes economic disaster.

"Dramatic restructuring" through the introduction of district-wide choice means more than making a few changes within the existing system. It means the construction of *a new kind of public school system* that is capable of providing increased educational accountability, equity, and diversity, and is based upon a broader definition of educational excellence.

Under the traditional administrative structure of local public school districts, important decisions such as the district's philosophy of education, the organization and structure of its schools, the curriculum that will be taught, and the schools children will attend are made at the top by the school board or central administration. Decisions are then passed down to principals, teachers, students, and parents. The traditional structure prescribes in varying degrees where teachers and principals can and cannot work, what they will teach, and how they will teach it. The structure also determines how schools will be organized and operated, how students will be evaluated and graded, and how teachers and principals will be evaluated and promoted.

The introduction of districtwide choice, on the other hand, brings with it diversity in philosophy, curriculum, instruction, and evaluation. Decision making is invested in the clients of the district (parents and students) and in the professional staffs of the district's individual schools (teachers and principals). Instead of a top-down organization, choice encourages a bottom-up organizational framework. This does not mean that school boards and central administrators disappear in districts that have implemented systemwide choice, but it does mean that the traditional roles are radically changed. As

Rhoda Schneider, former commissioner of education in Massachusetts, concludes:

> We are convinced that the best education occurs when those nearest to the student make the key decisions about how they will learn. That is why, over recent years, we have developed an extensive program of support for urban schools, providing parent choice on the basis of different approaches to education. . . . Our commitment in Massachusetts has been to make schools different in focus but equal in quality and to give all parents the opportunity and the information to make significant choices for their children. . . . The programs funded under Chapter 636 to permit several hundred urban schools to develop distinctive approaches to educational leadership has come—as it should be—largely from the school level. In this process the role of the central administration has been to orchestrate diversity, to assure that the common educational goals of the school system are met, even if in many different ways. (1986, not paginated)

"To orchestrate diversity" rather than dictate uniformity is one of the most important changes and new roles local school districts must take as they begin restructuring through the process of choice. As Mary Anne Raywid observes:

> Clearly, we must call a halt to our century-long march toward standardization. . . . The evidence supporting such a strategy is extensive, varied, and certainly not new; we know for a fact that different youngsters learn in different ways and according to different patterns. When we persist in imposing a single instructional approach on all children, we succeed with some students and systematically handicap others. There is no reason (beyond our own perversity) to continue to assume that some single "right" approach exists that will suit every student. (1987, p. 766)

The introduction of choice forces a district's central administration to reorganize itself so that a great deal of the decision-making power is placed at the level of individual schools. The reorganization, however, must be done in such a way that clearly defines those powers (philosophical, curricular, instructional, staff selection, governance, and financial) that are the province of individual schools and those powers (collective bargaining, school construction, district fiscal responsibility, and district admission and transfer policy for desegregation purposes) that are the province of the central administration.

The new administrative structure must also make possible a form of individual school governance that empowers parents, teachers, and older students to play a major role in all school-level decision making. The new administrative structure must also provide a districtwide system of accountability in addition to the basic accountability provided by parents' and teachers' ability to abandon schools they perceive to be of low quality or unsuitable for their children or unsuitable to teach in. There must be an accountability system that can assess and chart the progress, or lack of it, in all schools.

Accountability must also include a more complex and challenging definition of what constitutes success for individual students. Performance on norm-referenced standardized tests should not be the sole criterion for determining academic success or failure. Students should be assessed in terms of whether they can think critically and actually *do* something with the material taught at school. Students should be expected to perform "real world" tasks, as in Lowell's microsociety school, rather than simply checking off answers to multiple choice questions. Assessment instruments like comprehensive records and portfolios should be introduced to allow students to demonstrate mastery and application of various skills. St. Paul Open School, an alternative public school in St. Paul, Minnesota, has used portfolios instead of course grades and test scores to assess student mastery of high school graduation requirements for more than 20 years.

Perhaps the most interesting aspect of the new administrative structure is the revamping of the central administration's department of curriculum and instruction. Traditionally, this department has had the task of deciding what will be taught in all district schools at each grade level. The staff of curriculum and instruction departments is usually made up of subject matter specialists. These specialists, together with teachers, develop a "scope and sequence" for each subject's content grade by grade, along with recommended ways for teaching it and for testing student achievement. These processes are issued in curriculum guides, which teachers and principals are required to follow.

This top-down imposition of control and uniformity over what is taught and how it is to be taught is a formidable obstacle to change and innovation in any school system. In most cases, reformers must find ways to circumvent these established rules and procedures. In East Harlem, Deborah Meier and a group of teachers, with the encouragement of then district superintendent Anthony Alvarado, were able to ignore the stated goals of the New York City school system to establish Central Park East Elementary School in 1974. The curriculum guides and other rules and regulations of the central administration and state education hierarchy were bypassed in what is called "creative obedience" in East Harlem.

Instead of trying to fit all students into a traditional school that focused on skill acquisition by breaking learning into discrete bits and pieces, Meier and her colleagues wanted to offer an alternative, open education approach. According to Meier:

> We were looking for a way to build a school that would offer youngsters a deep and rich curriculum that would inspire them with the desire to know: that would cause them to fall in love with books and with stories of the past; that would evoke in them a sense of wonder at how much there is to learn. . . .
>
> We also saw schools as models of the possibilities of democratic life. Although classroom life could certainly be made more democratic than traditional schools allowed, we saw it as equally important that the school life of *adults* be made more democratic. It seemed unlikely that we could foster democratic values in our classrooms unless the adults in the school also have significant rights over their workplace. (1987, pp. 754–755; emphasis in original)

The result was a school that became so successful that it has been cloned twice and expanded to include a high school component that has become a participant in Theodore Sizer's Coalition of Essential Schools. The latter accomplishment is all the more remarkable considering that according to regulations of the New York City school system, community school districts are not supposed to administer high schools.

Although East Harlem, through "creative obedience," has successfully overcome top-down administrative regulations and attempts to standardize education, it still finds itself at odds with a series of curricular mandates from the New York Board of Regents (New York's state board of education). These mandates contained in the Regents Action Plan spell out the required courses for students and the standardized norm-referenced tests of student performance in those required courses. The effect is the creation of a compulsory statewide curriculum that, according to Meier, ". . . leaves far less room for initiative and innovation at the school level" (1987, p. 757).

The attempt to standardize education and mandate school reform from the top down has consistently resulted in failure to improve students' academic performance. Edward Pauly concludes that reform proposals have failed because "researchers looked for the best curriculum, the best textbook, the best instructional method, the best kind of teacher, in the hope that once found, these solutions would make the schools work better" (1991, p. 2).

If restructuring is to bring about successful school improvement, schools will need to move away from uniformity and standardization and embrace, according to Pauly, a pluralistic policy. "Pluralistic policy explicitly abandons the search for the one best method that will fix everything. Instead it puts school officials and specialists at the service of teachers, students, and parents" (1991, p. 14). The introduction of choice and the development of a diversity of approaches and programs to fit the needs of every child would be examples of a pluralistic policy.

To introduce a pluralistic policy, district and state offices of curriculum and instruction will need to undergo radical change. Instead of telling individual schools or individual school systems what they must teach and how they must teach it, central curriculum and instruction offices at the district and state levels must become "offices of school development" charged with the task of assisting individual schools to become what they want to become.

These new offices of school development will not be staffed with subject matter specialists but with people who have a broad knowledge of different kinds of schools and programs. True diversity requires a wide range of alternatives that include traditional options like fundamentals and "back to basics," as well as more progressive options like Montessori, open education, and microsociety. Staff in the new offices of school development will have the expertise to provide technical assistance to individual schools as they develop new, comprehensive educational approaches and thematic and specialized programs.

This is the kind of administrative structure currently being developed in Lowell. Every school in the district is a school of choice and has been charged with the task of developing its own distinctive specialized program to be determined by the school's parents, teachers, and principal. Program facilitators, who have replaced subject matter coordinators in the central office, are assisting individual schools in their development and adoption of new magnet programs. These program facilitators are specially trained individuals who are assigned to a group of five or six schools. The facilitator may or may not be familiar with the particular specialized program selected by a school. If not, she or he will bring in resource people who have the knowledge and experience in the selected area.

Lowell is further institutionalizing its decentralized decision-making process by having each of the district's 28 schools develop a school-site management council that is responsible for spelling out the school's educational philosophy, its innovative curriculum, organizational pattern, and the development of staff and parent involvement strategies. The council also has a say in the staff selection process. The combination of a new central office of school development with a school-site management council at each school is a major step along the road to both educational diversity and accountability and to a truly equitable public education system.

AMERICA 2000

While school improvement and educational restructuring are underway in a number of local school districts and individual states around the country, the Bush administration has been busy offering its own vision of the "dramatic restructuring" of public education.

In 1991 President Bush and Secretary of Education Lamar Alexander released the U.S. Department of Education document *America 2000: An Education Strategy.* The document is the most significant assertion of a federal role in and a federal responsibility for public education since the Elementary and Secondary Education Act of 1965. *America 2000* attempts to be a national strategy for achieving educational excellence in four areas: "1. For today's students, 2. For tomorrow's students, 3. For those of us already out of school and in the work force, 4. For schools to succeed" (U.S. Department of Education, 1991, p. 12).

It is not our intent to analyze *America 2000* in great detail in this chapter, but we would like to discuss two of the document's strategies that relate to school choice. We would also like to comment on what we see as a glaring internal contradiction in the document's approach to school improvement and educational restructuring.

The first strategy would allow federal Chapter 1 monies to follow a student to any public or nonpublic school he or she chooses to attend. Putting aside the whole discussion of the appropriateness of spending public tax dollars to support private schools, we fail to see how such a plan would be of any benefit to children who qualify for Chapter 1 monies. The federal expenditure for each Chapter 1 student is less than $1,000. Private schools charge considerably more than that in tuition. Prestigious private schools cost between $10,000 and $15,000 and less prestigious private schools between

$5,000 and $10,000. Providing a family with $1,000 towards the cost of a private school education is of little value unless the family has the ability to supplement Chapter 1 monies. Because only poor families are eligible for Chapter 1 monies, it is unlikely they would have the necessary resources to take advantage of the option.

The second strategy would encourage states and local school districts to develop voucher plans that would permit students to attend both sectarian and nonsectarian private schools at public expense. These plans would provide families with a credit (voucher), probably in the amount of the annual state or local per pupil expenditure. Families could then apply the credit toward the tuition of a private school of their choice.

A few voucher plans already exist around the country, but they have typically been designed for special underserved populations and apply only to students attending nonsectarian private schools. In Vermont 95 communities do not have public high schools. Consequently, these communities may designate a public or private nonsectarian school in an adjacent town as the tuition school for its students. Tuition is then paid for by the resident community to the designated tuition school. Some communities do not designate a tuition school, leaving students free to attend public or private schools of their choice. Reimbursement from the resident community, however, is limited to the average per pupil cost in the state. Maine has similar provisions for high school students in some 30 towns throughout the state (City Club of Chicago, 1989).

A much-publicized voucher plan passed by the Wisconsin state legislature in 1990 provided a limited number of economically disadvantaged students in the Milwaukee public schools with a voucher worth $2,500 to attend private nonsectarian schools during the 1990–91 school year. Eight schools agreed to accept the vouchers and enroll 400 students. Three hundred forty-one students actually enrolled. Eighty-two were forced to leave when two schools dropped out of the plan. One of these schools went bankrupt and closed; the other resumed religion classes and chose to leave the plan. Two hundred fifty-nine students remained in the plan at the end of the 1990–91 school year (Kantrowitz & Barrett, 1991). At the beginning of its second year of operation (1991–92) Milwaukee's voucher plan enrolled 560 students in seven private schools.

The voucher proposal in *America 2000* is much more ambitious and is a greater threat to public education because it would provide monies to allow all parents, advantaged as well as disadvantaged, to choose among sectarian and nonsectarian schools. We believe the ultimate effect of the proposal would be to provide further incentive and a large subsidy for middle- and upper-class parents to abandon the public schools.

Voucher plans do not provide full reimbursement for private school tuition. Families have to make up the difference between the tuition of the private school and the value of the voucher. Few poor families have the necessary means to do so, while many middle- and upper-class families do. As we indicated earlier, less prestigious private schools have tuition costs of $5,000–$10,000. A voucher based on the annual per pupil expense of a local school district might at best be worth $3,000–$4,000, which still falls short of most private schools' tuition costs. Vouchers thus end up being a subsidy for those middle- and upper-class families that can afford to make up the difference between private school tuition costs and the value of the voucher. Clearly, the result is further inequity in public education.

Our final objection to *America 2000*'s voucher proposal is that it is not designed to promote school improvement. It is designed to be an escape mechanism for families that wish to abandon the public schools and can afford to do so. Families who leave the public schools and enroll their children in private schools have little or no incentive to improve public education. They also have little or no incentive to provide tax support for the public schools their children no longer attend. It does not take much imagination to envision American education divided into two separate, unequal, and de facto racially and economically segregated school systems as a result of the expansion of vouchers.

The promotion of nonpublic school choice is a major flaw in *America 2000*, but we are even more troubled by an internal contradiction that runs throughout the document. On the one hand, *America 2000* argues for making the school the site of reform; because, in the document's words, "real education improvement happens school by school, the teachers, principals, and parents in each school must be given the authority—and the responsibility—to make decisions about how the school will operate" (U.S. Department of Education, 1991, p. 23). Yet, its method for determining "real education improvement" is to apply top-down national standards, to be assessed by national examinations.

The very act of setting national goals (the document identifies six) continues the idea set forth some 10 years ago in *A Nation at Risk* (National Commission on Excellence in Education, 1983) that there are mutually agreed upon national standards for subject matter content and student performance for which all Americans should be held accountable. *America 2000* identifies subject matter content in five areas: math, science, English, geography, and history. "World Class Standards" for each of the subjects are to be developed that "represent what young Americans need to know and be able to do if they are to live and work successful in today's world" (U.S. Department of Education, 1991, p. 21).

To measure student progress towards reaching these "World Class Standards," new "American Achievement Tests" will be developed and administered at grades 4, 8, and 12. While the tests will be voluntary, colleges will be urged to use them for admissions and businesses for hiring. As a reward, citations will be given to high school students who perform well on the tests. To receive federal assistance, states and local school districts must adopt the national goals and strategies put forth in the document.

This entire process of identifying standards and testing for their achievement is clearly aimed at encouraging the formation of a uniform, standardized, national curriculum that all schools will feel compelled to follow and implement. Indeed, the President's Advisory Committee on Educational Policy, a group of leading educators and businessmen called together to advise the administration, has told the president that a national curriculum and national testing should be developed and imposed on all schools.

How can schools be the sites of reform if they must accept these "World Class Standards" and implement the new "American Achievement Tests"? What becomes of teachers and principals who wish to practice in, and all those parents who wish their children to attend, schools where content is not structured into subject matter compartments of science, math, English, geography, and history? What becomes of open education, Montessori, continuous progress, whole language, and microsociety schools? What happens to the many teachers, principals, and parents who believe that children should not be subjected to norm-referenced standardized testing? As Deborah Meier points out:

> We cannot achieve true reform by fiat. Giving wider choices and more power to those who are closest to the classroom are not the kinds of reforms that appeal to busy legislators, politicians, and central board officials. They cannot be mandated, only facilitated. Such reforms require fewer restraints, fewer rules—not more of them. They require watchfulness and continuous documenting and recording, not a whole slew of accountability schemes tied to a mandated list of measurable outcomes. (1987, p. 757)

The central question to be asked regarding the "dramatic restructuring" of public education is, Who is going to make the decisions about what our public schools will be like? Who will decide what schools will teach, how they will be organized, the role students and parents will play in school governance, and how success and failure will be measured?

Where in *America 2000* are the voices of teachers and principals in the public schools, the people who have the job of making education happen and are given insufficient resources and support to do it? Where are the voices of parents? Do parents want federal authorities and national education experts to make basic decisions about what their children will learn and when they will learn it? What about the students, parents, teachers, and administrators in our urban public school systems? How do they feel about meeting "World Class Standards" in the five subject areas and taking "American Achievement Tests" to monitor their progress?

THE FUTURE OF PUBLIC EDUCATION

As discussed earlier in this chapter, top-down national goals, a standardized curriculum, standardized norm-referenced tests, and vouchers that encourage middle- and upper-class parents to abandon the public schools are not the answer to improving public education in America. The answer, we believe, begins with the creation of a new organizational structure for our public school systems, a structure based upon the deliberate and conscious creation of a broad range of diverse instructional and curricular approaches to schooling to fit the enormous diversity of our students. It includes both parental and professional choice of those diverse schools, the individual school autonomy necessary to make that educational diversity possible, and the guaranteed provision of genuine educational equity for *all* students.

Such diversity and choice not only can be applied to entire schools and school systems but also can be extended down to the level of individual classrooms within schools. While teachers and students may have chosen a particular school because of the suitability of its educational program, the organization of classes and classrooms within the school may or may not suit the particular interests or learning styles of those individual teachers and students. Both teachers and students should therefore be able to have a degree of control over who inhabits those classes and classrooms, in order to ensure a good and workable match between who is teaching and who is learning.

The new structure of diversity, parental and professional choice, individual school autonomy and equity permits us to adopt quite a different approach to children and schooling, an approach best characterized by psychologist Howard Gardner:

> The single most important contribution education can make to a child's development is to help him toward a field where his talents best suit him, where he will be satisfied and competent. We've completely lost sight of that. Instead, we subject everyone to an education where, if you succeed, you will be best suited to be a college professor. And we evaluate everyone according to whether they meet that narrow standard of success.
>
> We should spend less time ranking children and more time helping them to identify their natural competencies and gifts and cultivate those. There are hundreds and hundreds of ways to succeed and many different abilities that will help you get there. (quoted in Goleman, 1986, p. 23)

Such a new structure must also provide an adequate system of accountability, a mechanism that can ensure we are educating our children and young people as they should be and need to be educated. The accountability system begins with the fact that parental choice provides an almost automatic method of determining whether a school is providing the quality parents want. If parents do not believe a school is providing both the kind and quality of education they want for their children, they can select another school that does meet those needs. Similarly, teachers who feel a school is not providing them with professional satisfaction can ask for a transfer. Any school that is abandoned by both parents and teachers is clearly a school that, at the very least, needs to be revamped and, if necessary, reopened as a brand-new school designed better to serve those parental and professional standards of quality.

We see the adoption of public school choice as the first necessary step in the creation of a restructured and improved public education system in this country. Such improvement, however, will happen only if our public schools are arranged so that everyone in them—students, parents, teachers, principals, central administrators, school board members, indeed the entire community—is empowered to play a meaningful role in the educational process.

Public education has for too long imposed upon people a vision of teaching and learning that is authoritarian rather than democratic. As Lowell superintendent George Tsapatsaris has observed:

> In a democracy, you can't just tell people what's good for them and then impose it on them whether they want it or not. Yet that's what we have always done in public education. . . .
>
> We are all individuals. We learn and work in different ways. If you give students, teachers, and principals a chance to learn and work in an environment they prefer—a place they have chosen of their own free will, where they feel comfortable and respected—we think they will direct their energies towards a common goal: excellence. (1985, p. 10)

Parent Survey

Dear Parents and Guardians:

The _____ Public Schools are now embarked upon a community-wide planning process to make the public schools of this city into a national model for what the American public school system should become in the years ahead. This process will be successful only if everyone in _____ becomes part of the process. This means that all parents must be involved in making all of the important decisions about what the _____ Public Schools will be like in the 21st century.

In order for all parents to become involved, we are asking you to tell us the kinds of kindergarten through grade 5 elementary schools you would like your children to go to. We want you to tell us what those different kinds of schools are. We then want you to be able to choose to have your children attend the schools you want.

The different kinds of educational options you want at the elementary school level will be carried through the middle and high school levels. You will thus be able to have the kind of schooling you want for your children all the way from kindergarten through high school. We want *every* elementary, middle, and high school in _____ to become a school of choice. A school of choice is a school that:

- Offers a particular kind of schooling and/or offers a special curriculum that parents want for their children and which parents and students can then choose.
- Teaches all of the basic skills of reading, writing, and mathematics but in special and different ways.
- Voluntarily attracts both minority and nonminority students. In order to guarantee that all _____ public schools will be desegregated, all admissions to schools of choice are carefully controlled so that minority isolation in the school system is reduced and eventually eliminated.

- Maintains all existing special programs such as Chapter 1, bilingual education, special education, physical education, music, and art.
- Has the strong involvement of parents.

You are not at this time being asked to sign your child up for any school of choice. However, in planning for schools of choice we need to know the different kinds of schools and special programs you would like to have for your children in the _____ Public Schools.

The parents of the children in the _____ Public Schools have helped in the preparation of this survey by suggesting the different kinds of educational programs that might make schools of choice attractive to parents and students in _____. The five different kinds of schools and four special themes listed below are the kinds of educational programs offered in other school systems in the state.

Please read the following descriptions of possible schools of choice and possible curricular themes and follow the directions on each page. If you need or would like any help in filling out this survey form, please call _____.

Sincerely,

*   *   *

On the following pages you will find descriptions of five different kinds of elementary schools, different educational philosophies, different ways for children to learn, and ways schools can be organized and run. Please write the number "1" on the line next to the description of the kind of school you would most like your child to attend. Write the number "2" on the line next to the program that would be your second choice, the number "3" in the box next to your third choice, and so on to number "5". You may make a single selection for all of your children, or you may fill out a separate form for each of your children if you would like a different educational program for each of them.

_____ *A Traditional School*

This school concentrates on teaching students the basic skills of reading, writing, arithmetic, and responsibility. The school emphasizes discipline and order. Parents and teachers work together to guarantee that the school has high academic standards and that all students are doing their best to work at or above grade level.

____ *A Continuous Progress School*
This school encourages students to progress through a carefully defined academic curriculum at their own best rate of speed. Children are able to advance as fast as possible in each subject area and may be working at different grade levels in different subjects.

____ *A Developmental School*
This school stresses the intellectual, social, physical, and moral development of each child. As students participate in activities that help them learn about objects, ideas, other children, and adults, they learn to teach themselves and work independently in specially designed learning centers.

____ *A Montessori School*
This school provides students with a carefully organized sequence of learning activities using specially designed learning materials which students are free to work with on their own. The curriculum is based on the idea that children are naturally curious, want to learn, and like to work with materials and on projects that interest them.

____ *A Microsociety School*
This school is designed to help students learn how a democratic, free market society works. Students set up and run their own society in school, including their own legislature and governmental system, their own courts and judicial system, their own banks and businesses, their own newspapers and publishing businesses. Students learn all their basic skills by actually using them in the operation of their society.

Next you will find descriptions of four specialized programs that any of the different kinds of schools previously described could also have. For instance, a traditional school might also have a special curriculum devoted to fine and performing arts or to science and technology. A continuous progress school might also offer a special two-way bilingual curriculum.

If you would like one or all of your children to have such a specialized program, please put a "1" on the line next to the one you would like most, a "2" on the line next to your second choice, and so on to number "4."

____ *A Science and Technology Program*
This program will concentrate on the study of, and offer students the opportunity to work on special projects in, oceanog-

raphy, biology, botany, astronomy, physics, and such modern
technology as computers and data processing.

____ *A Fine and Performing Arts Program*

This program will provide students with an opportunity to
develop their artistic skills both as artists and appreciators of
all the arts, including acting, painting, music, sculpture, theatre, and dance.

____ *A Multicultural Program*

This program offers students an opportunity to learn about
the languages and cultures that make up the modern world,
including a study of their own ethnic heritage and the ethnic
heritage of other students in the school.

____ *A Two-Way Bilingual Program*

This program offers students the opportunity to learn another
language in elementary school. English-speaking children will
learn Spanish, and Spanish-speaking children will learn English in mixed classes taught in both languages, beginning in
kindergarten.

____ *Other*

If none of the options described above is the one you want for
your child, please describe the school or program you want in
the space below.

In order to analyze the results of this survey, we need you to
provide the following information:

1. In order to have your child attend the school you have chosen for
   him or her, would you be willing to have him or her transported
   to school by bus, free of charge?
   ___ Yes   ___ No   ___ Maybe
2. If the school of your choice offered an extended day program
   starting before school and running until 4 or 5 o'clock in the
   afternoon, would this make you more interested in sending him
   or her to that school?
   ___ More   ___ Less   ___ Not
   Interested   Interested   Interested
3. What racial or ethnic group does your child/children belong to?
   Please check the correct line.
   ___ Black   ___ Native American
   ___ Hispanic   ___ Asian
   ___ White   ___ Other (please specify)

4. Names of the child/children for whom you are filling out this survey form.
Please print.

Name of Child	*Grade Level*	*Present School*

5. Name of parent or guardian filling out this form:

Address: _____

Telephone: _____

Please have your child/children return this completed survey form to their teacher at school by _____.

Professional Survey

Dear Teachers, Principals, and Staff:

The _____ Public Schools are now embarked upon a communitywide planning process to make the public schools of this city into a national model for what the American school system should become in the years ahead. This process will be successful only if everyone in _____ becomes part of the process. This means that all teachers, principals, and staff must be involved in making all of the important decisions about what the _____ Public Schools will be like in the 21st century.

In order for all professional staff to become involved, we are asking you to tell us the kinds of kindergarten through grade 5 elementary schools you would like to teach and work in. We want you to tell us what those different kinds of schools are. We then want you to be able to choose to teach and work in the schools you want.

We want *every* elementary, middle, and high school in _____ to become a school of choice. A school of choice is a school that:

- Offers a particular kind of schooling and/or offers a special curriculum that parents want for their children and which parents and students can then choose.
- Teaches all of the basic skills of reading, writing, and mathematics but in special and different ways.
- Voluntarily attracts both minority and nonminority students. In order to guarantee that all _____ public schools will be desegregated, all admissions to schools of choice are carefully controlled so that minority isolation in the school system is reduced and eventually eliminated.
- Maintains all existing special programs such as Chapter 1, bilingual education, special education, physical education, music, and art.

- Has a school-based management and decision-making organization, with teachers involved in all decisions.
- Has the strong involvement of parents.

You are not at this time being asked to sign up to teach in any of these schools of choice. However, in planning for schools of choice we need to know the different kinds of schools and special programs you would like to be able to teach and work in and, therefore, would like to have available to you in the _____ Public Schools.

Teachers, principals, and parents of the children in the _____ Public Schools have helped in the preparation of this survey by suggesting the different kinds of educational programs that might make schools of choice attractive to parents and students in _____. The five different kinds of schools and four special themes listed below are the kinds of educational programs offered in other school systems in the state.

Please read the following descriptions of possible schools of choice and possible curricular themes and follow the directions on each page.

Sincerely,

*   *   *

On the following pages you will find descriptions of five different kinds of elementary schools, different educational philosophies, different ways for children to learn, and ways schools can be organized and run. Please write the number "1" on the line next to the description of the kind of school you would like to teach in. Write the number "2" on the line next to the program that would be your second choice, the number "3" on the line next to your third choice, and so on to number "5", the one you would least like to teach in.

____ *A Traditional School*
This school concentrates on teaching students the basic skills of reading, writing, arithmetic, and responsibility. The school emphasizes discipline and order. Parents and teachers work together to guarantee that the school has high academic standards and that all students are doing their best to work at or above grade level.
____ *A Continuous Progress School*
This school encourages students to progress through a care-

fully defined academic curriculum at their own best rate of speed. Children are able to advance as fast as possible in each subject area and may be working at different grade levels in different subjects.

_____ *A Developmental School*

This school stresses the intellectual, social, physical, and moral development of each child. As students participate in activities that help them learn about objects, ideas, other children and adults, they learn to teach themselves and work independently in specially designed learning centers.

_____ *A Montessori School*

This school provides students with a carefully organized sequence of learning activities using specially designed learning materials which students are free to work with on their own. The curriculum is based on the idea that children are naturally curious, want to learn, and like to work with materials and on projects that interest them.

_____ *A Microsociety School*

This school is designed to help students learn how a democratic, free market society works. Students set up and run their own society in school, including their own legislature and governmental system, their own courts and judicial system, their own banks and businesses, their own newspapers and publishing businesses. Students learn all their basic skills by actually using them in the operation of their society.

Next you will find descriptions of four specialized programs that any of the different kinds of schools previously described could also have. For instance, a traditional school might also have a special curriculum devoted to fine and performing arts or to science and technology. A continuous progress school might also offer a special two-way bilingual curriculum.

If you would like the school you work in to have such a specialized program, please put a "1" on the line next to the one you would most want, a "2" on the line next to your second choice, and so on to number "4", the one in which you would least like to work.

_____ *A Science and Technology Program*

This program will concentrate on the study of, and offer students the opportunity to work on special projects in, oceanography, biology, botany, astronomy, physics, and such modern technology as computers and data processing.

—— *A Fine and Performing Arts Program*
This program will provide students with an opportunity to develop their artistic skills both as artists and appreciators of all of the arts, including acting, painting, music, sculpture, theatre, and dance.

—— *A Multicultural Program*
This program offers students an opportunity to learn about the languages and cultures that make up the modern world, including a study of their own ethnic heritage and the ethnic heritage of other students in the school.

—— *A Two-Way Bilingual Program*
This program offers students the opportunity to learn another language in elementary school. English-speaking children will learn Spanish, and Spanish-speaking children will learn English in mixed classes taught in both languages, beginning in kindergarten.

—— *Other*
If none of the options described above is the one you want to teach and work in, please describe the school or program you want in the space below.

In order to analyze the results of this survey, we need you to provide the following information:

1. In order to teach in the school you have selected, would you be willing to ask for a voluntary transfer to that school?
   —— Yes   —— No   —— Maybe

2. Present school and grade level you are teaching in:
   _____

3. What racial or ethnic group do you belong to? Please check the correct line.
   —— Black   —— Native American
   —— Hispanic   —— Asian
   —— White   —— Other (please specify)

4. Your name: _____

   Address: _____

   Telephone: _____

   Please return this completed survey form to your principal by
   _____.

"Controlled" Admissions and Transfer Policy

ELEMENTS OF THE PLAN

This policy is designed to provide maximum choice for parents in selecting the schools their children will attend, within the constraints imposed by the available space, the requirements of racial balance, and the special needs of children. It provides stability of assignment for children and, at the same time, a mechanism for adjusting the racial balance of the schools, as needed, without unnecessary movement of students. It gives priority in assignment to current residents of the city over later arrivals.

1. EARLY REGISTRATION AND ASSIGNMENT

There will be two major registration periods for parents of preschool children. Parents will be encouraged to register their children in the fall of the year prior to the year the children are expected to enter kindergarten. At the end of the registration period, assignments will be made, with parents being given a reasonable period of time to indicate that they will accept the assignment.

In the spring of each year there will be a second registration period. At that time, parents whose children received assignments the previous fall will be asked to reconfirm their intention of having their children attend the _____ Public Schools in the fall. This will eliminate holding space for children from families whose plans have changed, and will facilitate the spring assignments.

Every effort will be made to ensure that all parents know about the early registration and the procedures involved. There will be announcements in the press and other media, notices through the school to parents who may have younger children, and announcements to all preschools, daycare centers, and community organizations. The Parent Information Center, public library, and all relevant staff will have the information parents need. Parents will be encouraged to visit the schools that might interest them prior to registration, in order to make informed choices.

2. LONG-RANGE ASSIGNMENT POLICY

Students currently in the public schools: The school to which a student is assigned as of September, 19__ will become his or her "home school," with the exceptions listed below. Every effort will be made to allow the student to remain in the home school until graduation. Each student is *guaranteed* that he or she will not be moved for desegregation purposes for at least 4 years.

New and transferring students: Students newly entering the school system, those whose parents' request for a transfer has been approved, and those subject to reassignment as defined in the sections below will all be assigned to the nearest "appropriate school." All such assignments will be made by the central assignment officer in the Office of Desegregation. Once the assignment is made, that school will become the student's "home school."

3. CRITERIA FOR ASSIGNMENT.   The criteria for assigning students will be defined as follows:

Parental preference: At the time of registration, or at the time a transfer is requested, a parent may indicae three or more preferences in order of importance to the parent. These may include a parent's desire that the child attend the nearest possible school and/or that siblings be assigned together. Every effort will be made to accommodate parents' preferences within the system of priorities established in this policy. If it is not possible, for any reason, to grant one of the parent's first three choices, and the parent has reason to be dissatisfied with the child's assignment, that parent may file an appeal under the provisions of section 7: "Hardship Appeals."

Space available: Space available in a particular school, program, or grade will be defined according to the policy then in effect as to class size and school capacity, so long as it does not disrupt existing classes.

Special-needs students: Any student requiring a bilingual program will be assigned to such a program, regardless of other provisions of this policy. A student requiring a special education program will be assigned according to the Core Evaluation process, regardless of other provisions of this policy. A student who has completed a bilingual program, or a student once classified as 502.4 who is reclassified as 502.3, will be allowed to complete one additional "transitional year" in the same school, after which the student will be subject to reassignment under the assignment policy. The exception will be that any student who completes his or her "transition year" in the 7th grade will be allowed to complete the 8th grade without transfer. Once it becomes possible to establish sites for both special and bilingual education students in more schools throughout the system, the provisions for transfer may no longer be necessary.

Racial balance: Transfers and new assignments, except as noted above, must meet the requirements of racial balance. The goal is to achieve a majority/minority percentage within each school, program, and grade that reflects, within a few percentage points, the majority/minority percentages of the school system as a whole.

Accordingly, minority students only will have the right of assignment to a school, program, or grade having a minority population below 30 percent. Majority students only will have the right of assignment to a school, program, or grade having a minority population over 50 percent. Minority and majority students may both apply to schools, programs, and grades that are racially balanced.

In the event that there are more applications to a racially balanced school, program, or grade than can be accommodated in the available space, priority will be determined as follows: If the minority population is 5 percent or more *above* the systemwide average, priority will be given to majority students; if it is five percent or more *below* the systemwide average, priority will be given to minority students.

Sibling preference: Between two students otherwise equally eligible for a single space, the one whose parents have indicated a sibling preference, if any, will have priority.

Place of residence: The final criterion to be considered, all other priorities being equal, is that the student living nearest to the school will have priority.

Lottery: In the event that, after considering all priorities, there are still more students eligible for particular choices than there are spaces available in that school, program, or grade, The Office of Desegregation will conduct a lottery of those in the relevant categories (i.e., minority 3rd graders, or majority 5th graders, or whatever category might apply), in order to fill the available space. Other applicants, to the extent possible, will be granted their other choices.

Waiting list: A parent whose child cannot, for any reason, be assigned to the school, program, or grade of his or her first choice may have the child's name placed on a waiting list for the first suitable vacancy. Pupils on the waiting list will have priority, in case of an available vacancy, over new entrants to the school system.

Magnet schools and programs: Applications for magnet schools and programs must meet the same criteria as other applications. The application procedure is the same. The parent may indicate the desired magnet as a preference. A committee representative of all magnets will work with the Office of Desegregation to ensure that magnet admissions meet the special requirements of each of the magnet schools and programs, as well as the general policy.

4. DISSEMINATION OF INFORMATION

Data on the space available and the racial balance of the schools and programs will be completed and published in October and March of each year. Information about the assignment policy and about the various schools and programs for which parents may apply will be circulated as widely as possible, on a regular basis. In addition to announcements in the press and other media, parents may seek assistance at the Parent Information Center, the schools, and the public libraries. Information will be provided in Chinese, English, French, Greek, Portuguese, and Spanish.

5. CERTIFICATION OF ADDRESS

All entering students and current students, upon request, must submit a properly documented Certification of Address form to the central assignment officer. A copy of a lease or mortgage, and/or a notarized signature of a landlord or manager of the property will constitute documentation. The central assignment officer will be responsible for verifying addresses as necessary.

6. TRANSFERS

Once a student has attended a school, a parent who is dissatisfied with the assignment may request a transfer. Except in the case of students needing bilingual or special education programs, no transfer will be made that violates racial balance, or to a school or program in which there is not sufficient space. A parent whose request for transfer is denied may file an appeal under section 7: "Hardship Appeals."

If assignment to a particular school clearly creates an undue medical hardship for a student, and an assignment to a different school would lessen the hardship, a parent may apply for a transfer for medical reasons. Such a request must be accompanied by a statement from the child's physician and a statement from an official of the _____ Public Schools. Such cases may be investigated by the Office of Desegregation and reviewed by the _____ Public Schools physician.

Students who move from one address to another within the school system will *not* be required to transfer to another school. However, the parent of such a student may request a transfer, and the student will be reassigned under the provisions of the "Long-Range Assignment" policy.

Under special and rare circumstances transfers may be made by the school system when proof of the necessity can be provided by a parent, school official, or other relevant professional (e.g., social worker, probation officer). Such cases will be reviewed by the Office of Desegregation, and the transfer can be made only if the need is clearly substantiated.

7. HARDSHIP APPEALS

A parent whose child has not been assigned to one of the first three preferences and who is dissatisfied with the assignment received, and one whose request for transfer has been denied, may file a hardship appeal, as follows:

Step 1: The parent fills out the Hardship Appeals form, submits it, along with related information and documentation, to the Office of Desegregation. The Office of Desegregation will make a finding of fact, after any necessary investigation, including consultation with the parent(s) and other knowledgeable or relevant individuals. The findings, all information, and the recommendations of the Office of Desegregation will be forwarded within 5 working days to the Hardship Appeals Board. A copy of the findings and recommendation will be sent to the parent making the appeal.

Step 2: The Hardship Appeals Board will review each case referred to it. Using the criteria of safety and extraordinary educational need, the board will recommend approval or disapproval of the request in writing, giving the reasons for the recommendation.

Step 3: The superintendent, the chairperson of the Hardship Appeals Board, and a representative of the Office of Desegregation will review each case. Unless there are compelling reasons against such actions, the recommendation of the board will be implemented. An example of a compelling reason would be documented and substantial reason to doubt the facts as presented.

In any case, the final decision, along with the recommendations of the board and superintendent, will be conveyed to the parent(s) in writing by the Office of Desegregation. Every effort will be made to expedite the work of the Hardship Appeals Board, so that final decisions can be made within 2 weeks of the board's receipt of an appeal, or prior to the opening of school in the case of appeals received during the summer.

Proceedings of the Appeals Board will be recorded by a secretary, and all records will be maintained accurately. They will be available for review by members of the School Committee and authorized representatives of the State Department of Education. Records will not be made public, but public disclosure may be made of statistics relating to hardship appeals, provided always that the identity of appellants is protected.

Composition of the Hardship Appeals Board:
Central Office administrator (chairperson)
Bureau of Pupils Services representative
Teacher (designated by Teachers' Association)
Two parents (one majority, one minority recruited by the Office of Desegregation)
Resident of _____ representing religious, human, or social services.

Parent Information Center

1. *What is the Parent Information Center?*
   The Parent Information Center is the place where parents come to find out about the schools in _____ and to register their children for a school of their choice. The Center also offers programs of interest to parents at various times during the year.

2. *Do I need to come to the Center to register my child for school?*
   Yes. If you have a child in kindergarten through grade 8 and are new to the system, you will need to come to the Center to register these children.
   Yes. If you are interested in any of the Early Childhood programs offered by the _____ Public Schools, you will need to come to the Center to request a place in these programs.
   Yes. If you have moved within the city, you will need to come to the Center to change address so that appropriate school and transportation arrangements can be made for your children.
   No. If you have a child who is a high school student you should go directly to the Registration Center at the high school.

3. *What do I have to bring with me when I come to register my child?*
   You need to bring a copy of your child's shot (immunization) record, evidence of your child's date of birth, proof of your current address (rent or mortgage receipt, utility bill), a transfer slip from your child's previous school, and a notarized Certificate of Address (this form is available at the Center). If you do not speak English at home, you will need to bring your child with you, so the staff at the Center can give the child a language test.

4. *How long will it take to register my child?*
   During most of the year it will usually take less than 30 minutes to register your child for school. During the busiest times of the year—from August 15 to September 15, and during kindergarten registration in March—you may have a much longer wait.

5. *What school may my child attend?*
   You will be asked to choose three schools in the zone in which

you live that you would like your child to attend. There are two zones in the city.

6. *How will I know about the schools my child can attend?*

   There are many ways in which you can learn about the schools your child can attend. The staff at the Center knows much about the schools and can speak to you about them in Khmer, Lao, Spanish, and Portuguese, as well as English. School profiles in many languages can be found at the Center. Tours of the schools in which you are interested can also be easily arranged.

7. *Who will decide which school my child attends?*

   School assignments are done by the student assignment officer, whose office is at the Center. Most children—more than 95%—are assigned to one of their parents' first three school choices. If it is not possible to meet any of your requests, you will be asked to make further choices. Any child not assigned to a first-choice school is automatically placed on a waiting list for that school. If it is not possible to place your child in your first-place school and you feel the school assignment has been very difficult for you, you are encouraged to write a letter explaining this difficulty to the Parent Appeal Board.

8. *How will my child get to school if the school is not near my house?*

   _____ Public Schools will provide transportation by yellow school bus for your child. Your child will receive a bus pass within 3–4 days of the school assignment. This pass will tell you at what time and at what place the bus will pick up your child.

9. *Can my child be transported from a babysitter's or day care provider's home?*

   If your babysitter/day care provider lives in the same zone in which you live, special arrangements can be made with the Transportation Office to have your child picked up and dropped off at the babysitter's or day care provider's home.

10. *How long will it take before I know which school my child will be attending?*

    Most of the time, you will know which school your child will be attending before you leave the Center. If your child needs to be placed in a Special Education classroom, it will take longer.

11. *Will all of my children be able to go to the same school?*

    Every effort is made to keep families together when school assignments are made.

12. *Can I transfer my child from one school to another?*

    Yes. You may request a transfer of school for your child at any time during the school year.

    If you have not moved, your child's name will be placed on a waiting list for your first-choice school.

If you have moved within the zone your child is currently attending school, you may choose to have the child remain in the school he or she is attending, or you may request a different school.

If you would like your child to attend a different school during the next school year, you must come to the Center after May 1 and request this change.

13. *How long is the waiting list?*

Because there are individual waiting lists for each school, it is difficult to say how long a child must wait before being placed in a first-choice school. Waiting lists are reviewed weekly after October 15. Parents are notified by telephone or mail when seats become available.

14. *Should I become involved with the school my child attends?*

Parent involvement in their children's schools is encouraged by _____ Public Schools. Parents are the first teachers their children have. Parents know their children's needs better than anyone else and, because of this, are aware of how the school can best meet these needs.

15. *How can I become involved in my child's school?*

You may become involved in many ways. You may wish to go on field trips. You may want to become active in the school's parent group. You may want to help in classrooms or the library. You might like to represent your child's school on a citywide level. Because many of the staff members at the Parent Information Center are familiar with the Citywide Parent Council and parent groups within each school, they can provide you with information about the groups and the names of people you can contact.

Schools of Choice/School Improvement Planning Form

**TO ASSIST PRINCIPAL/TEACHER/PARENT TEAMS
IN EXISTING ELEMENTARY SCHOOLS THAT ARE
INITIATING A SCHOOL OF CHOICE/SCHOOL
IMPROVEMENT PLANNING PROCESS**

School District: _____

School: _____

Principal: _____

School Address: _____

Telephone: _____

Present Minority/Majority Ratio   *Desired Ratio*
   ___ % Minority   ___ % Minority
   ___ % Majority   ___ % Majority

I. What would we like our school to be like 5 years from now? What will be its distinctive quality, its special attractiveness that will make other parents want to send their children to this school and will make other teachers and principals want to come to work here? What is our definition of educational "excellence"?

   A. *Educational Philosophy*: What do we think public schooling should be about? What do we want the educational goals of this school to be? What kind of school do we wish to become?

   B. *Curriculum*: What do we think this school should teach and children should learn, and do we think we should specialize in a particular area of the curriculum?

   C. *School Organization*: How should our school be organized in order to implement the educational philosophy and curriculum described above? This would include grade structure, classroom organization such as age-graded, self-contained, or continuous progress. What should the school's schedule be?

D. *Testing and Reporting to Parents*: How should the educational progress of children be assessed? What kinds of tests should be used? How often should they be administered? What kinds of report cards should be used and how often?

E. *Behavior and Discipline Code*: What should the school's discipline code be? How should it be administered?

F. *Governance*: What should the governance structure of the school be? What roles should the principal, teachers, parents, and students have in making important decisions about the school? What kinds of control should the school have over its budget?

G. *Parent/Community Involvement*: How should parents and community people be involved in the life of the school and in the educational program?

H. *Evaluation*: How do we wish the school and its educational program to be evaluated? How should that evaluation be conducted? What criteria should be used, and what criteria should not be used?

II. What do we propose to do to ensure that the poor and minority children in our school have equal educational opportunity, that they have equal access to all programs and resources, and that they are not segregated into lower level classes or tracks?

III. In order to implement the educational program described above, how do we see our present school facility being used 5 years from now?

A. Present Use of Facility
   1. Number of full-sized classroom spaces contained in building ___
   2. Auxiliary Spaces
      Auditorium ___
      Library ___
      Gym ___
      Cafeteria ___
      Combination of above ___
      Principal's Office ___
      Teachers' Room ___
      Parents' Room ___
      Other (specify) ___

3. Full-Sized Classroom Spaces Now Being Used for Specialized Purposes
   Library ⎯⎯
   Art ⎯⎯
   Music ⎯⎯
   Science Lab ⎯⎯
   Computer Lab ⎯⎯
   Industrial Arts ⎯⎯
   Home Economics ⎯⎯
   Other (specify) ⎯⎯

4. Present Use of Classroom Spaces

Mainstream Classes		*Average Class Size*
Prekindergarten	⎯⎯	⎯⎯
Kindergarten	⎯⎯	⎯⎯
1st Grade	⎯⎯	⎯⎯
2nd Grade	⎯⎯	⎯⎯
3rd Grade	⎯⎯	⎯⎯
4th Grade	⎯⎯	⎯⎯
5th Grade	⎯⎯	⎯⎯
6th Grade	⎯⎯	⎯⎯
7th Grade	⎯⎯	⎯⎯
8th Grade	⎯⎯	⎯⎯
Nonmainstream Classes		*Average Class Size*
Bilingual	⎯⎯	⎯⎯
Special Needs	⎯⎯	⎯⎯
Chapter 1	⎯⎯	⎯⎯

Total Present School Population ⎯⎯
Mainstream Average Class Size ⎯⎯

B. Proposed Use of Facility 5 Years from Now

Mainstream Classes		*Average Class Size*
Prekindergarten	⎯⎯	⎯⎯
Kindergarten	⎯⎯	⎯⎯
1st Grade	⎯⎯	⎯⎯
2nd Grade	⎯⎯	⎯⎯
3rd Grade	⎯⎯	⎯⎯
4th Grade	⎯⎯	⎯⎯
5th Grade	⎯⎯	⎯⎯
6th Grade	⎯⎯	⎯⎯
7th Grade	⎯⎯	⎯⎯
8th Grade	⎯⎯	⎯⎯

Nonmainstream Classes   *Average Class Size*
Bilingual   ____   ____
Special Needs   ____   ____
Chapter 1   ____   ____
Full-Sized Classroom Spaces to Be Used for Specialized Programs
Library ____
Art ____
Music ____
Science Lab ____
Computer Lab ____
Industrial Arts ____
Home Economics ____
Other (specify) ____
Total Proposed Maximum School Enrollment ____

IV. In order to implement the educational program described above, what will we need in the way of additional staff and resources over the next 5 years?

A. Additional Full-Time Staff

_____

B. Additional Part-Time Staff

_____

C. Curriculum and Staff Development Workshops
   1. Workshops During School Year
      No. of Workshops ____
      How Often ____
      No. of Staff Involved ____
   2. Workshops During Summer
      No. of Workshops ____
      How Often ____
      No. of Staff Involved ____
D. Technical Assistance (Consultants)
   1. During School Year
   2. During Summer Workshops
E. Equipment
F. Materials and Supplies
G. Auxiliary Services (field trips, etc.)
H. Staff Travel
Total Cost of Additional Staff and Resources ____

V. In order to have the kind of school we want 5 years from now, what additional resources do we need during the coming school year, and what would they cost?

A. Additional Full-Time Staff Cost

_____ ____

B. Additional Part-Time Staff

_____ ____

C. Fringe Benefits for Above ____

D. Curriculum and Staff Development Workshops

   1. Workshops During School Year

      No. of Workshops ____

      How Often ____

      No. of Staff Involved ____

   2. Workshops During Summer

      No. of Workshops ____

      How Often ____

      No. of Staff Involved ____

E. Technical Assistance

F. Equipment

G. Materials and Supplies

H. Auxiliary Services

I. Staff Travel

Total Cost of Additional Resources ____

References

Across the nation. (1988, October 19). *Education Week*, p. 2.

Across the nation. (1990, April 25). *Education Week*, p. 15.

Allen, J. (1988, October 24). Improving education: Lessons from the states. *The Heritage Foundation State Backgrounder*, pp. 1–11.

Alves, M. J., & Willie, C. V. (1987). Controlled choice: An approach to effective school desegregation. *The Urban Review, 19*(2), 67–88.

Arnove, R., & Strout, T. (1978). Alternative schools: Cultural pluralism and reality. *Educational Research Quarterly, 2*(4), 75–95.

Blank, R. K. (1984). The effects of magnet schools on the quality of education in urban school districts. *Phi Delta Kappan, 66*(4), 270–272.

Carnegie Council on Adolescent Development. (1989). *Turning points: Preparing American youth for the 21st century.* Washington, DC: Author.

Carnegie Forum on Education and the Economy. (1986). *A nation prepared: Teachers for the 21st century.* New York: The Carnegie Corporation.

Carnegie Foundation for the Advancement of Teaching. (1988). *An imperiled generation: Saving urban schools.* Princeton, NJ: Princeton University Press.

Cavazos, L. F. (1989). *Educating our children: Parents and schools together.* Washington, DC: U.S. Department of Education.

Choice spurs debate at NEA representative assembly. (1989, September). *ISTA Advocate*, pp. 4, 14.

Chubb, J. E. (1989). Making schools better: Choice and educational improvement. *Equity and Choice, 5*(3), 5–10.

Chubb, J. E., & Moe, T. M. (1990). *Politics, markets, and America's schools.* Washington, DC: Brookings Institution.

City Club of Chicago. (1989). *Educational choice: A catalyst for school reform. A report of the task force on education.* Chicago: Author.

Citywide Educational Coalition. (1985). *A study of attitudes among parents of elementary school children in Boston.* Boston: Martilla & Kiley Associates.

Clewell, B. C., & Joy, M. F. (1990). *Choice in Montclair, New Jersey: A policy information paper.* Princeton, NJ: Educational Testing Service.

Clinchy, E. (1989). Public school choice: Absolutely necessary but not wholly sufficient. *Phi Delta Kappan, 71*(4), 289–294.

Clinchy, E. (1989). *Planning for schools of choice: Achieving equity and excellence.* Andover, MA: New England Center for Equity Assistance.

Clinchy, E. (1991). America 2000: Reform, revolution, or just more smoke and mirrors? *Phi Delta Kappan, 73*(3), 210–218.

Coleman, J. S. (1987). Families and schools. *Educational Researcher, 16*(7), 32–38.

Colorado Department of Education. (1990). *Report to the Colorado general assembly.* Denver: Author.

Colorado Department of Education. (1991). *Report to the Colorado general assembly.* Denver: Author.

Diegmueller, K. (1991, November 27). Budget concerns spur lawmakers to reconsider choice law in Mass. *Education Week*, pp. 1, 19.

Domanico, R. J. (1989). *Model for choice: A report on Manhattan's district 4.* New York: Center for Educational Innovation, Manhattan Institute for Policy Research.

Doyle, D. P., & Levine, M. (1984). Magnet schools: Choice and quality in public education. *Phi Delta Kappan, 66*(4), 265–270.

Elam, S. M., Rose, L. C., & Gallup, A. M. (1991). The 23rd annual Gallup poll of the public's attitudes towards the public schools. *Phi Delta Kappan, 73*(1), 41–56.

Erickson, D. A. (1982). *The British Columbia story: Antecedents and consequences of aid to private schools.* Los Angeles: Institute for the Study of Private Schools.

Finn, C. (1989). The problem: A depressing look at education in America today. In *The right to choose: Public school choice and the future of American education.* New York: Center for Educational Innovation, Manhattan Institute for Policy Research.

Fiske, M. C. (1990, Winter). A modest proposal to divest ourselves of the burden, both moral and economic, of our derelict public schools in a global yard sale. *Smith Alumnae Quarterly*, pp. 19–20.

Fleming, P. S., Blank, R. K., Dentler, R. A., & Baltzell, D. C. (1982). *Survey of magnet schools: Interim report for the U.S. Department of Education.* Washington, DC: James H. Lowry & Associates.

Foley, E. M., & Crull, P. (1984). *Educating the at-risk student: More lessons from alternative high schools.* New York: Public Education Association.

Foley, E. M., & McConnaughy, S. B. (1982). *Towards school improvement: Lessons from alternative high schools.* New York: Public Education Association.

Freedberg, L. (1990, September 18). Schools struggle to finance reform. *The San Francisco Chronicle*, pp. A1, A6.

Fund, J. H. (1990, September 4). Milwaukee's schools open—to competition. *The Wall Street Journal*, p. A10.

Gold, M., & Mann, D. W. (1984). *Expelled to a friendlier place: A study of effective alternative schools.* Ann Arbor: University of Michigan Press.

Goleman, D. (1986, November 9). Rethinking the value of intelligence tests. *The New York Times Educational Life Supplement*, p. 23.

Grant, G. (1988). *The world we created at Hamilton High.* Cambridge, MA: Harvard University Press.

Gregory, T. B., & Smith, G. R. (1987). *High schools as communities: Small schools reconsidered.* Bloomington, IN: Phi Delta Kappa Educational Foundation.

Hughes, L. W., Gordon, W. M., & Hillman, L. W. (1980). *Desegregating America's schools.* New York: Longman.

Jennings, L. (1989, March 8). In poll, slim majority of board chiefs oppose choice. *Education Week*, p. 5.

Jones, J. D. (1988). The six school complex. *Equity and Choice, 4*(2), 31–38.

Kantrowitz, B., & Barrett, T. (1991, May 27). A real test for vouchers. *Newsweek*, pp. 60–61.

Kearns, D. T., & Doyle, D. P. (1991). *Winning the brain race. A bold plan to make our schools competitive.* San Francisco: Institute for Contemporary Studies.

Kirkpatrick, D. W. (1990). *Choice in schooling.* Chicago: Loyola University Press.

Larson, J. C., & Allen, B. A. (1988, January). *A microscope on magnet schools, 1983 to 1986. Vol. 2: Pupil and parent outcomes.* Rockville, MD: Montgomery County Public Schools.

Lieberman, M. (1989). *Privatization and educational choice.* New York: St. Martin's Press.

McPherson, J. (1990). 2 of 3 school superintendents non-supportive of "choice." Unpublished manuscript, Central Washington University, Ellensburg, WA.

Meier, D. (1987). Central Park East: An alternative story. *Phi Delta Kappan, 69*(10), 753–757.

Meier, D. (1991, March 4). Choice can save public education. *The Nation*, pp. 266–271.

Metz, M. H. (1986). *Different by design: The context and character of three magnet schools.* New York: Routledge & Kegan Paul.

Minnesota open-enrollment program has had mixed impact, survey says. (1991, February 27). *Education Week*, p. 24.

Moore, D. R., & Davenport, S. (1989). High school choice and students at risk. *Equity and Choice, 5*(1), 5–10.

Most Minnesota students transfer for convenience, survey shows. (1990, February 21). *Education Week*, p. 2.

Nathan, J. (1988). Who benefits from options in urban education? *National Center on Effective Schools Newsletter, 3*(2), 9–11.

Nathan, J. (Ed). (1989). *Public schools by choice.* St. Paul, MN: The Institute for Learning and Teaching.

Nathan, J. (1989a). Helping all children, empowering all educators: Another view of school choice. *Phi Delta Kappan, 71*(4), 304–307.

Nathan, J. (1989b). *Progress, problems, and prospects of state educational choice plans.* Washington, DC: U.S. Department of Education, Office of Planning, Budget & Evaluation.

Nathan, J. (1989c). Progress, problems, and prospects with state choice plans. In J. Nathan (Ed.), *Public schools by choice* (pp. 203–224). St. Paul, MN: The Institute for Learning and Teaching.

Nathan, J., & Jennings, W. (1990). *Access to opportunity: Experiences of Minnesota students in four statewide school choice programs 1989-90.* Minneapolis: Center for Social Change.

National Coalition of Advocates for Children. (1985). *Barriers to excellence: Our children at risk.* Boston: Author.

National Commission on Excellence in Education. (1983). *A nation at risk.* Washington, DC: U.S. Government Printing Office.

National Governors' Association. (1986). *Time for results: The governors' 1991 report on education.* Washington, DC: Center for Policy Research and Analysis.

National Panel on High School and Adolescent Education. (1976). *The education of adolescents: The final report and recommendations.* Washington, DC: U.S. Government Printing Office.

Newmann, F. M. (1989). Reducing student alienation in high school: Implications of theory. In L. Weis, E. Farrar, & H. G. Petrie (Eds.), *Dropouts from school: Issues, dilemmas and solutions* (pp. 153–177). Albany: State University of New York Press.

New York State Education Department. (1985). *New York state magnet school research study.* Albany: MAGI Educational Services.

Panel on Youth of the President's Science Advisory Committee. (1974). *Youth: Transition to adulthood.* Chicago: University of Chicago Press.

Pauly, E. (1991). *The classroom crucible.* New York: Basic Books.

Pavuk, A. (1987, April 22). Catholic schools continue slide in enrollment. *Education Week*, p. 9.

Pearson, J. (1989). Myths of choice: The governor's new clothes? *Phi Delta Kappan, 70*(10), 821–823.

Perhaps the single most promising reform idea. (1989, January 18). *Education Week*, p. 24.

Peterkin, R. S., & Jones, D. S. (1989). Schools of choice in Cambridge, Massachusetts. In J. Nathan (Ed.), *Public schools by choice* (pp. 125–148). St. Paul, MN: The Institute for Learning and Teaching.

Rand Corporation. (1981). *A study of alternatives in American education: Vol. 7. Conclusions and policy implications.* Santa Monica, CA: Author.

Raywid, M. A. (1981). The first decade of public school alternatives. *Phi Delta Kappan, 62*(8), 551–557.

Raywid, M. A. (1982). *The current status of schools of choice.* Hempstead, NY: Project on Alternatives in Education.

Raywid, M. A. (1987). Public choice, yes; vouchers, no! *Phi Delta Kappan, 69*(10), 762–769.

Raywid, M. A. (1989). The mounting case for schools of choice. In J. Nathan (Ed.), *Public schools by choice* (pp. 13–40). St. Paul, MN: Institute for Learning and Teaching.

Report on educational clinics: Program years 1982–1984. (1985). Olympia, WA: Legislative Budget Committee (Report to Washington State Legislature).

Research and Policy Committee of the Committee for Economic Development. (1988). *Investing in our children.* Washington, DC: Committee for Economic Development.

Richmond, G. (1973). *The micro-society school: A real world in miniature.* New York: Harper & Row.

Rinehart, J. R., & Lee, J. F. (1991). *American education and the dynamics of choice.* New York: Praeger.

Ross, E. (1991, September 9). New Massachusetts school-choice program gets a mixed reception. *The Christian Science Monitor*, p. 11.

Rothman, R. (1990, March 7). Choice claims overstated, A.S.C.D. panel concludes. *Education Week*, p. 8.

Schmidt, P. (1991, May 1). Budget deficit spurs district in California to close its schools. *Education Week*, pp. 1, 14.

Schneider, R. (1986, May 5). Keynote address at the Conference on Diversity and Choice, Worcester, MA.

Smith, G. R., Gregory, T. B., & Pugh, R. C. (1981). Meeting student needs: Evidence for the superiority of alternative schools. *Phi Delta Kappan*, *62*(8), 561–564.

Snider, W. (1987, June 24). The call for choice. *Education Week*, pp. C1–24.

Snider, W. (1989, November 11). Known for choice, New York's district 4 offers a complex tale for urban reformers. *Education Week*, pp. 1, 13.

Snider, W. (1989, December 13). California district makes choice initiative centerpiece of plan to reinvigorate schools. *Education Week*, pp. 1, 22.

Snider, W. (1990, March 27). Voucher system for 1,000 pupils adopted in Wis. *Education Week*, pp. 1, 14.

Soglin, A. (1990, March 7). Segregation reduced in most schools. *West County Times*, Richmond, CA. p.1A.

Steinbach, C., & Pierce, N. R. (1989, July 1). Multiple choice. *National Journal*, *21*(26), 1692–1695.

Thompson, S. D. (1989, April 19). Improvement threatened by "stampede" for choice. *Education Week*, pp. 32, 34.

Tsapatsaris, G. (1985). How we magnetized a city school system. *Principal*, *64*(3), 8–10.

Uchitelle, S. (1978, April). *Policy implications for school districts affording public school options: A case study of results of school choice in one community.* Paper presented at the annual meeting of the American Educational Research Association, Toronto.

U.S. Department of Education. (1989). *Improving schools and empowering parents: Choice in American education.* Washington, DC: Author.

U.S. Department of Education. (1991). *America 2000: An education strategy.* Washington, DC: Author.

Walberg, J. W., Bakalis, M. J., Bast, J. L., & Baer, S. (1989). Reconstructing the nation's worst schools. *Phi Delta Kappan*, *70*(10), 802–805.

Young, T. (1990). *Public alternative education. Options and choice for today's schools.* New York: Teachers College Press.

Index

About the Authors

Timothy W. Young is Professor of Education at Central Washington University, where he teaches undergraduate methods and graduate foundations courses. He received his doctorate in secondary education from Indiana University in 1980. Previously, he was a social studies and English teacher for 6 years.

Professor Young has written numerous articles on teaching and learning in *Action in Teacher Education, American Secondary Education, Journal of Classroom Interaction,* and *Phi Delta Kappan.* His primary interest is alternative schools. His book, *Public Alternative Education: Options and Choice for Today's Schools,* was published by Teachers College Press in 1990.

Evans Clinchy is Senior Field Associate at the Institute for Responsive Education (IRE) in Boston. Previously he served as program officer and editorial director at Educational Facilities Laboratories, coordinating director of the Elementary Social Studies Program at Educational Services Inc., director of the Office of Program Development of the Boston Public Schools, and president of Educational Planning Associates.

Mr. Clinchy has assisted many school systems around the country in the development of magnet schools, "controlled" choice desegregation, and systemwide school improvement plans. He is a contributing editor of the IRE journal *Equity and Choice* and has written numerous articles for that publication as well as for *Phi Delta Kappan* and other educational journals.